This catalogue is made possible in part by a grant from the Jeffersonian Restoration Advisory Board, which since 1984 has played a leading role for the University of Virginia in securing support for the restoration of Jefferson's Academical Village.

THOMAS JEFFERSON'S ACADEMICAL VILLAGE  **THE CREATION OF AN ARCHITECTURAL MASTERPIECE**

THOMAS JEFFERSON'S ACADEMICAL VILLAGE

THE CREATION OF AN ARCHITECTURAL MASTERPIECE

RICHARD GUY WILSON, Editor

Contributors:

PATRICIA C. SHERWOOD

JOSEPH MICHAEL LASALA

RICHARD GUY WILSON

JAMES MURRAY HOWARD, AIA

BAYLY ART MUSEUM OF THE UNIVERSITY OF VIRGINIA
Charlottesville

Distributed by
UNIVERSITY PRESS OF VIRGINIA
Charlottesville and London

This book was published in conjunction with the exhibition
Thomas Jefferson's Academical Village: The Creation of an Architectural Masterpiece,
organized by the Bayly Art Museum, October 7, 1993–January 9, 1994.

ISBN 0-8139-1511-2

Designed by Gibson Parsons Design.
Printed and bound in the United States of America.

Cover: detail of fig. 42.
Inside front and back covers: aerial view of The Lawn. (Photograph by Robert Llewellyn.)
Frontispiece: Rotunda from the South. (Photograph by Bill Sublette.)
Contents page: Thomas Sully (American, 1783-1872), *Thomas Jefferson*, 1822, oil on canvas,
102¼ by 66 inches. The West Point Museum Collections, United States Military Academy, West Point, New York.

Library of Congress Cataloging-in-Publication Data

Jefferson, Thomas, 1743–1826.
  Thomas Jefferson's academical village : the creation of an architectural masterpiece / Richard Guy Wilson,
      editor ; with contributions by Patricia C. Sherwood, Joseph M. Lasala, James Murray Howard.
          p.   cm.
      "Published in conjunction with the exhibition ... organized by the Bayly Art Museum,
          October 7, 1993–January 9, 1994"—T.p. verso.
          Includes bibliographical references and index.
          ISBN 0-8139-1511-2
  1. Jefferson, Thomas, 1743–1826—Exhibitions. 2. Architectural drawing—19th century—
      Virginia—Charlottesville—Exhibitions. 3. Neoclassicism (Architecture)—Virginia—
  Charlottesville—Exhibitions. 4. University of Virginia—Buildings—Exhibitions. 5. Charlottesville
              (Va.)—Buildings, structures, etc.—Exhibitions.
  I. Wilson, Richard Guy, 1940– . II. Sherwood, Patricia C. III. Lasala, Joseph M. (Joseph Michael)
      IV. Howard, James Murray, 1947– . V. University of Virginia. Art Museum. VI. Title.
NA2707.J45A4   1993
727'.3'02222—dc20   93-21324
                                                                                    CIP

CONTENTS

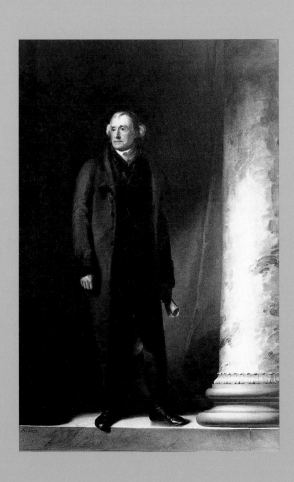

FOREWORD

This book, published to coincide with an exhibition of the same name at the Bayly Art Museum, grows out of the University of Virginia's celebration of the 250th anniversary of Thomas Jefferson's birth. The Museum's staff had long sought a way to participate meaningfully in the anniversary, and when this project was suggested by two distinguished faculty members, Richard Guy Wilson, Commonwealth Professor of Architectural History in the University's School of Architecture, and Charles Brownell, now of Virginia Commonwealth University, it was clear that the right vehicle had been found. Striking new research produced by two of their former students, Joseph Michael Lasala and Patricia C. Sherwood, seemed an ideal basis on which to build one of the most complex exhibition and publishing projects in the history of the Bayly Art Museum.

Jefferson first stated his views on the importance of public education during the 1770s, when he was a member of the Virginia House of Delegates. In this commitment, he was far ahead of his time, and he never wavered. It was only after he retired to Monticello at the close of his presidency, however, that he was able to invest himself fully in creating one of his proudest accomplishments, the University of Virginia. This book deals with the evolution of his ideas for the University, the exchanges he had with friends and the contributions they made, the way in which his views on public education and architecture came together, the pervasive impact his creation had on subsequent American architecture, and the ways in which the University is coming to terms with issues of conservation regarding historic buildings that are still in use. Such rich material offers virtually unlimited potential for research, and the authors do not wish to suggest that the book or exhibition are exhaustive in their treatment of these subjects. The exhibition includes less than half of Jefferson's surviving drawings, and certainly it only begins to address comparative materials. Nevertheless, the project marks an important step forward in our understanding of the Academical Village.

In order for such a large project to come to fruition, the help of many people is required. First, one must recognize the significant contributions to scholarship made by the authors, Richard Guy Wilson, Joseph Michael Lasala, Patricia C. Sherwood, and James Murray Howard. In particular, the efforts of Professor Wilson, who worked long hours over many months while serving as guest curator and editor, deserve special notice.

The exhibition's success required the cooperation of Alderman Library's Special Collections Department, for that is where most of Jefferson's drawings for the University customarily reside. Fifty of these most precious works are on view; never before have so many of the original drawings been lent to one exhibition. We extend our warm thanks to Edmund Berkeley, Jr., Director of Special Collections, and particularly to Kathryn N. Morgan, Curator of Rare Books, and Michael F. Plunkett, Curator of Manuscripts, for their extraordinary generosity and helpfulness. We also must express our gratitude to Gregory A. Johnson, Senior Public Services Assistant in the Special Collections Department, and to the Photographic Services Department at the Library for responding to our numerous requests.

At the Museum, Suzanne Foley, Curator, has shouldered with her usual aplomb the enormous organizational burden a project of this magnitude creates. In this effort she has been ably assisted by Nancy Eklund, Allyson Petty, and Janet Hayden. Kurt G. F. Helfrich, working with Professor Wilson, provided exemplary research assistance. The Museum's Administrator, Ruth Cross, handled the endless financial arrangements, while the Executive

Secretary, Susan Howell, provided services too numerous to mention. Jean Lancaster Collier, Registrar, and Rob Browning, Preparator, were instrumental in making the exhibition a reality.

The necessary funds could not have been raised were it not for the efforts of Cecilia Minden Cupp, the Museum's Director of Development. She worked in concert with Jeffrey Plank and Nicholas Duke, Director and Associate Director of Corporate and Foundation Relations, respectively, in the Office of University Development; Leonard Sandridge, Executive Vice President; and Colette Capone, Associate Vice President and Director of the Budget. The Design Committee of the Jeffersonian Restoration Advisory Board provided substantial financial support at a critical juncture. We hope this publication justifies their confidence and that it ably serves the goals to which they have devoted so much over the years. Robert Sweeney, Vice President for Development, proved an enthusiastic supporter. For additional financial support the Museum is indebted to Harry Porter, Dean, and the Dean's Forum of the School of Architecture, and to the Committee for the Commemoration of Thomas Jefferson's 250th Birthday. We are grateful also for the sponsorship of the following individuals and corporations, who have recognized the important benefits the arts provide in the communities they serve: Reid and Jessica Nagle, Merrill Lynch & Co., Inc., Davenport & Co. of Virginia, and Stubblefield Full Service Photo Lab.

The Director of the University Press of Virginia, Nancy Essig, supported the publishing project through several incarnations. Bill Sublette, Editor of the *Alumni News*, cheerfully provided numerous photographs of the University in response to exacting standards and tight deadlines.

We gratefully acknowledge the Museum's Volunteer Board, led by Punkie Feil, for its unwavering support. We also extend warmest thanks to the superb volunteers who, under the direction of a tireless and enthusiastic chair, Marjorie Burris, organized the Museum's 1993 Benefit, the proceeds of which were dedicated to the exhibition.

Jim Gibson and Mary Alice Parsons of Gibson Parsons Design, Charlottesville, created an elegant design for the book and other printed materials; Jeff Bushman and several other members of the team at Bushman, Dreyfus Architects in Charlottesville produced an equally sensitive installation design. Thanks are also due George Cruger, whose gentle editing of the manuscript enhances every page of the book.

An advisory team assisted the principal researchers in the early phases of the project. In addition to the authors, this group included William Beiswanger, Architect at Monticello; Charles Brownell, Associate Professor of Art History at Virginia Commonwealth University; Omer A. Gianniny, emeritus Chair of the Humanities Division of the Engineering School; K. Edward Lay and Robert Vickery of the Architecture School; and Michael Plunkett.

Thanks also to the architectural historians, all long affiliated with the University of Virginia, who laid the foundations for the research presented here, particularly Fiske Kimball, Frederick D. Nichols, William B. O'Neal, and K. Edward Lay.

The Bayly Art Museum takes great pleasure and pride in presenting this work to the public. It is our hope that it stimulates further research into the origins and impact of Thomas Jefferson's Academical Village.

ANTHONY HIRSCHEL
Director, Bayly Art Museum

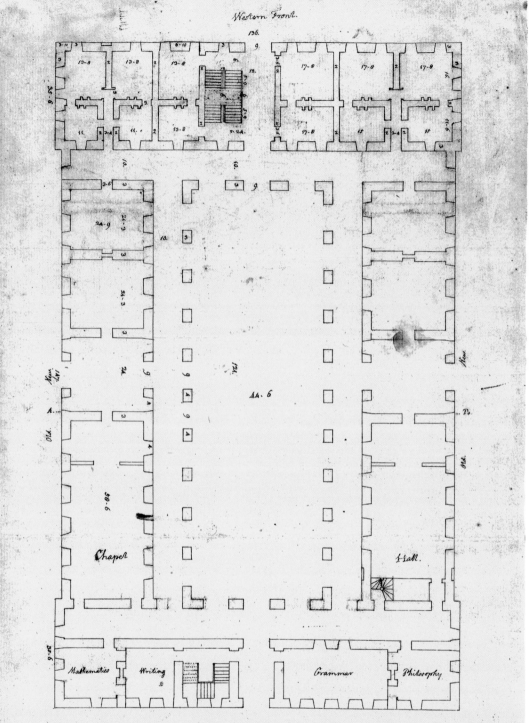

1. Thomas Jefferson. *Plan for an addition to the College of William and Mary…*, 1771-72. Ink on laid paper, 13⅝ x 9. N-421. The Huntington Library, San Marino, California.

NOTE ON CAPTIONS:
All measurements are in inches; height precedes width. N-numbers relate to checklist in Frederick Doveton Nichols, *Thomas Jefferson's Architectural Drawings*, (Charlottesville: Thomas Jefferson Memorial Foundation, 1961). "Special Collections" denotes Special Collections Department, University of Virginia Library. "Jefferson Papers" denotes Thomas Jefferson Papers, Special Collections Department, Manuscripts Division, University of Virginia Library.

EDUCATION AND ARCHITECTURE:
The Evolution of the University of Virginia's Academical Village

PATRICIA C. SHERWOOD and JOSEPH MICHAEL LASALA

Thomas Jefferson believed that education was the key to the survival of the new republic he had helped to frame in 1776. He reasoned that if the masses were educated they would be able to recognize tyranny in all its forms and thereby avoid its destructive forces. To this end, he championed a system of public education for Virginians, and the crowning achievement of his crusade was the establishment of the University of Virginia and the "Academical Village" he designed to house the institution.[1]

TO WATCH AND PRESERVE THE SACRED DEPOSIT

Jefferson's education, following the standards of an eighteenth-century Virginia family of landed gentry, began at home with a private tutor. At age nine he attended a Latin school and a few years later received a thorough grounding in the classics at a school in Albemarle County run by the Reverend James Maury. He learned to read both Greek and Latin fluently and deemed it a "sublime luxury" and a "rich source of delight."[2] When he was sixteen he entered the College of William and Mary in Williamsburg, Virginia, where he was exposed to the Enlightenment philosophies of one of the few instructors he admired, William Small. They regularly corresponded until Small's death in 1775. After two years at the College, Jefferson left to study law under George Wythe.[3]

Jefferson's architectural education also began in Williamsburg, where he purchased a treatise on classical architecture from a cabinetmaker near the college gate while he was still a student, thus beginning a love affair with architecture that he pursued and delighted in for the rest of his life.[4] This avocation attracted the attention of Lord Dunmore, Governor of the British Crown Colony of Virginia, and in 1771 or 1772 he asked Jefferson to design an addition to the main building of the College (fig. 1). Jefferson's plan was rooted in European tradition; in fact, completing the College's quadrangular arrangement had been the original intention when construction began in 1695. Though it had been rebuilt after a fire and a chapel had been added by 1732, the quadrangle had never been completed due to the lack of funding. Jefferson no doubt turned to one of the eighteenth-century Leoni editions of Andrea Palladio's *Four Books of Architecture* and chose one of the many palazzo forms illustrated there (fig. 2).[5] His scheme for a quadrangle with an interior arcade arranged around an open courtyard reappears in many of his later designs and would become a prime ingredient of his plan for the University of Virginia. The foundations of his addition to

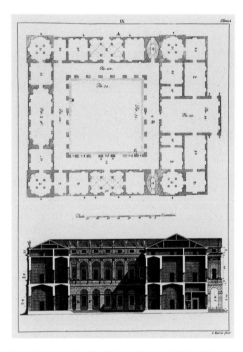

2. Andrea Palladio. "Building at Vicenza," Plate IX from Book II, Chapter 3 ("Construction of Houses in Towns"), Giacomo Leoni, *The Architecture of A. Palladio: In Four Books*, 3rd edition (London, 1742). Special Collections, Rare Books Division.

William and Mary were begun, but building activity was suspended in 1774 because of the troubles surrounding the impending Revolution.[6]

Jefferson himself best expressed the origin of the idea of public education in Virginia when he reminisced about the revised code of laws that

Wythe, Edmund Pendleton, and he had prepared for Virginia in 1776–79: "Nobody can doubt my zeal for the general instruction of the people. Who first started that idea? I may surely say myself. turn to the bill in the revised code which I drew more than 40. years ago; and before which the idea of a plan for the education of the people generally had never been suggested in this state."[7]

Jefferson described his "Bill for the More General Diffusion of Knowledge" as his "Quixotism," and as the most important of the 126 bills submitted to the Commonwealth in 1779.[8] The bill was structured around three tiers of education: elementary schools (primary level), district colleges (secondary level), and a university. It also included provisions for choosing school sites and building facilities for the primary and secondary levels. For the collegiate and university levels, it provided a selection process for educating the best and brightest students "without regard to wealth, birth or other accidental condition or circumstance."[9]

The primary level called for instruction in reading, writing, and arithmetic to "all the free children, male and female" for a period of three years at the public cost, and longer at their own expense, if so desired. It provided for a group of electors to choose a convenient site to build a "school house" for the "hundreds" (measured districts within each county), to keep it in good repair, and when needed to build another in the same place or somewhere else convenient to the hundred.[10] The idea of convenience implies two things: centrality and impermanence. The building type for primary schools was always a log school house, and a central location was a prime ingredient in all of Jefferson's plans for educational institutions.[11] Virginia's widely dispersed agrarian population and primitive transportation required convenient and accessible facilities if these educational proposals were to reach everyone as Jefferson envisioned.

The collegiate level would include among its subjects Greek, Latin, and higher mathematics. In describing the facilities for these schools, Jefferson became more specific, writing that "the said overseers shall forthwith pro-

ceed to have a house of brick or stone for the said grammar school, with necessary offices, built on the said lands, which grammar school-house shall contain a room for the school, a hall to dine in, four rooms for a master and usher, and ten or twelve lodging rooms for the scholars."[12] Again, the location would be central, but Jefferson specified one large building for all facilities, as was characteristic of educational institutions at that time.

The highest level of studies would be at the College of William and Mary. The most advanced educational institution in Virginia, it contained six professorships, including one for teaching Greek and Latin (a grammar school, academically the secondary level), one for teaching the Native Americans (a missionary school), two for divinity, and two for philosophy or the more advanced branches of science. Jefferson wrote a second bill that would eliminate the ecclesiastical nature of the College and expand the number of professorships to eight. He wished to render this institution "more useful" and make it an incubator where "the future guardians of the rights and liberties of their country may be endowed with science and virtue, to watch and preserve the sacred deposit." Other proposals would, if adopted by the Virginia Legislature, make William and Mary a true university.[13] His "Quixotic" scheme advocated cutting across all social and economic barriers to produce an educated elite of the best and brightest minds in the Commonwealth at the public expense. Lifting a bright young man above the station of his father and rendering him a protector of the new democracy was revolutionary, and Jefferson's ideas were far ahead of his contemporaries.

All of Jefferson's education bills initially fell on fallow ground, but in 1779 during his tenure as governor he took part in reforms at William and Mary that eliminated the grammar school and the two divinity schools.[14] They were replaced by "a professorship of law (Mr. Wythe), another of medicine, anatomy, chemistry and surgery (McLurg) and a third of modern languages, (Bellini)."[15] These changes, only a fraction of the reforms envisioned in Jefferson's original scheme, nevertheless shifted the College toward the seminary of science he had intended.

While serving as Minister to France from 1784 to 1789, Jefferson had an opportunity to observe various European educational systems, and advised a friend against sending America's youth there for higher education, stating that the disadvantages "would require a volume." He felt that in Europe young Americans would learn unsavory vices and a fondness for aristocracy, and would obtain knowledge useless for maintaining government at home. In defense of an American education, he wrote: "cast your eye over America: who are the men of most learning, of most eloquence, most beloved by their country and most trusted and promoted by them? They are those who have been educated among them, and whose manners, morals and habits are perfectly homogeneous with those of the country."[16]

In another letter from Paris, Jefferson compared the opportunity in America with that in Europe for educating the masses to maintain freedom:

If all the sovereigns of Europe were to set themselves to work to emancipate the minds of their subjects from their present ignorance and prejudices ... a thousand years would not place them on that high ground on which our common people are now setting out.... I think by far the most important bill in our whole code is that for the diffusion of knowledge among the people. No other sure foundation can be devised for the preservation of freedom, and happiness. If any body thinks that kings, nobles, or priests are good conservators of the public happiness, send them here.... Preach, my dear Sir, a crusade against ignorance; establish and improve the law for educating the common people.[17]

Jefferson's countrymen were not yet ready to listen, however, and only a shadow of his ambitious educational scheme passed in 1796, and that for primary schools only. The "Act to Establish Public Schools" proved totally ineffective due to the funding provisions.[18] By January 1800, Jefferson had also abandoned the hope that William and Mary would become the institution of his dreams. He wrote to Joseph Priestley: "We wish to establish in the upper country, and more centrally for the State, an University on a plan so broad and liberal and *modern*, as to be worth patronizing with the public support. The first step is to obtain a good plan: that is, a judicious selection of the sciences...." He went on to say that they planned to get the best possible professors from Europe who would in turn train their successors.[19] A few months later Jefferson wrote to Pierre Samuel DuPont de Nemours asking for curriculum recommendations, and in 1803 to M. Pictet concerning his plans to propose a university to the Virginia Legislature when the time was appropriate.[20]

The opportune time seemed to present itself late in 1804, when L.W. Tazewell solicited ideas from Jefferson to incorporate into a university proposal he and several other Delegates expected to submit to the next session of the Legislature. In Jefferson's reply, his concept for a grand seminary of learning for the useful sciences remained the same, but he had begun to think differently about the facilities to house the institution. He wrote with reference to the buildings:

... the greatest danger will be their overbuilding themselves by attempting a large house in the beginning, sufficient to contain the whole institution. large houses are always ugly, inconvenient, exposed to the accident of fire, and bad in cases of infection. a plain small house for the school & lodging of each professor is best. These connected by covered ways out of which the rooms of the students should open would be best. These may then be built only as they shall be wanting. in fact an University should not be an house but a village. this will much lessen their first expences [sic].[21]

By 1810 Jefferson had further developed this idea, and to the Trustees of a proposed college in Tennessee he explained that each professor's "small and separate lodge" should contain "only a hall below for his class, and two chambers above for himself; ... the whole of these arranged around an open square of grass and trees would make it, what it should be in fact, an Academical Village, instead of a large & common den of noise, of filth, & of

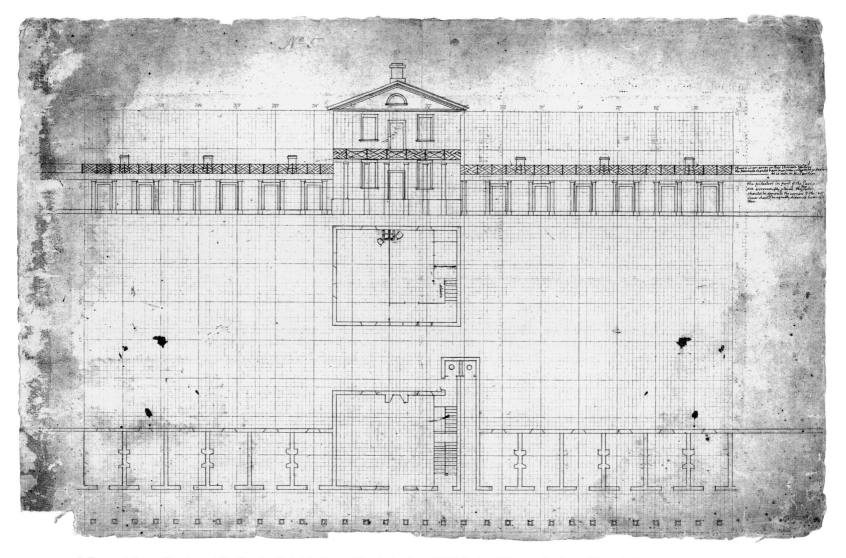

3. Thomas Jefferson. Elevation and Plan Showing Typical Pavilion and Dormitories, August 1814. Recto: pricking, scoring, iron-gall ink on laid paper, 13½ x 21. N-309. Jefferson Papers.

fetid air. It would afford that quiet retirement so friendly to study." He also suggested that the professors "might be at the head of their table if, as I suppose, it can be reconciled with the necessary economy to dine them in smaller & separate parties rather than in a large & common mess."[22] All that remained was the opportunity to transfer this mental blueprint to paper.

In 1809–10 the Legislature moved one step closer to an educational system in Virginia by setting up a Literary Fund for "the encouragement of learning." Funding would come from the sale of escheated or forfeited prop-

erty such as glebe lands confiscated from the Episcopal Church, fines, and various other sources. In the following session, Legislators voted to appropriate the money for the education of the poor.[23]

Jefferson continued to promote his educational ideas in correspondence and conversation with the myriad visitors who trekked to Monticello. In January 1814 he wrote to Dr. Thomas Cooper that he had "long had under contemplation and [had] been collecting materials for the plan of an university in Virginia.... This would probably absorb the functions of Wm. and Mary college, and transfer them to a healthier and more central position, perhaps to the neighborhood of this place [Monticello]."[24] Jefferson must have known that the opportunity to embark on his quest for a university in Virginia was finally at hand, for less than ten weeks later he was nominated to become a Trustee of the newly resurrected Albemarle Academy at the first meeting of its Board. This secondary school, which had been chartered by the state in 1803, had never been put into operation.[25] Peter Carr, Jefferson's nephew, was elected President of the Trustees at the next meeting, and Jefferson's son-in-law, Thomas Mann Randolph, was later elected to the committee charged with the task of petitioning the Legislature for funds arising from the sale of glebe lands to support the school.[26]

Jefferson's opportunity to translate his written concepts for a university into an architectural plan came in August 1814, when the committee assigned to secure a location for Albemarle Academy presented his plan at their meeting and recommended "its adoption by the Board as one best suited to the purpose, provided the work can be completed according to the terms of the estimate" (figs. 3 and 4).[27] Jefferson had drawn a plan almost identical to one he had described nearly ten years earlier to Tazewell. It contained nine identical pavilions flanked by ten dormitories on each side situated around three sides of a square and connected by covered walkways. In each of these small pavilions Jefferson provided a hall on the ground floor for instruction and two rooms upstairs for living quarters for the professors; it was very similar to the scheme described in 1810. He showed the dormitories fronted by a series of square brick piers crowned by a chinoiserie railing strongly resembling the treatment of the wings at Monticello (fig. 3). Designing for economy and expansion as needed, Jefferson had provided a simple and direct plan.

Apparently Jefferson did not intend for this plan to be just for the local Albemarle Academy, because in a letter written several weeks later to Carr, he explained: "On the subject of the academy or college proposed to be established in our neighborhood, I promised the trustees that I would prepare for them a plan, adapted, in the first instance, to our slender funds, but susceptible of being enlarged, either by their own growth, or by accession from other quarters." Noting his concept of a three-tier educational system, Jefferson explained that the Academy would begin with the general, or collegiate, level, and when possible would expand to the professional, or university, level. He listed nine professorships for the professional level, matching the number of pavilions on his ground plan, and architecture was among them.[28]

To further effect his intentions, Jefferson wrote a proposal for the Trustees to submit to the Legislature that would change the institution's name from Albemarle Academy to Central College. One of Jefferson's associates

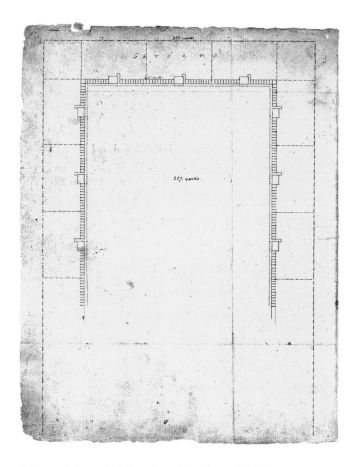

4. Thomas Jefferson. Preliminary Ground Plan, August 1814. Verso, detail: pricking, scoring, iron-gall ink on laid paper, 13½ x 21. N-309. Jefferson Papers.

later recalled the problem of choosing the name of the proposed college:

> *Mr. [Alexander] Garrett was one of the Trustees and together with his coadjudicators consulted Mr. Jefferson with regard to the course of instruction, organization &c. He [Jefferson] advised them to enlarge their plan and to establish a College. They agreed to it and proposed to call the institution 'Jefferson College.' Mr. Jefferson objected and said emphatically and repeatedly 'call it Central College.' His views prevailed and the Central College was founded.*[29]

The Trustees never made an attempt to operate Albemarle Academy under its original charter, and the bill for Central College was not submitted to the Legislature in 1815 as planned, due to the illness and death of Peter Carr. In January 1816, just before the bill was presented, Jefferson wrote to Colonel Charles Yancey, a Delegate from Albemarle County: "I recommend to your patronage our Central College. I look to it as a germ from which a great tree may spread itself."[30] The bill passed in February, providing for a board of six visitors empowered to raise money, in part, by subscription. One of the Albemarle Academy Trustees wrote to Governor Wilson Cary Nicholas recommending James Monroe, James Madison, Thomas Jefferson, John Hartwell Cocke, Joseph Carrington Cabell, and David Watson as Visitors (trustees): "That the first two named gentlemen will serve is presumed as they were inserted in the list at the instance of Mr. Jefferson."[31] Governor Nicholas appointed this distinguished Board of Visitors that fall, but their first official meeting did not occur until May 5, 1817.

The State Legislature also appropriated additional money for the Literary Fund that was owed to Virginia by the federal government. Governor Nicholas, one of the conservators of the fund, solicited Jefferson's advice on implementing an educational system that would best utilize the extra money. This gave Jefferson another opportunity to advance his personal agenda, and predictably he again proposed the three-tier system of public education. His letter makes clear that what he had designed for Albemarle Academy had been a "University Plan." In describing the pavilions, however, Jefferson mentioned for the first time a didactic function: "exhibiting models in architecture of the purest forms of antiquity, furnishing to the student examples of the precepts he will be taught in that art."[32]

To understand Jefferson's desire to build models of ancient architecture, one need only know that just as he had collected materials to help frame the best possible educational system for Virginia, he had also spent the past three decades attempting to reform Virginia's architecture. He believed that the best way to improve it was by education and by example. Since there were few chaste architectural models in Virginia to inspire him during his early years, he turned to architectural books to cultivate his design tastes. The books he first acquired, such as James Gibbs's *Book of Architecture* and *Rules for Drawing the Several Parts of Architecture*, and various editions of Palladio's *Four Books of Architecture*, espoused the beauty and harmony of ancient architecture and the methods one must follow in order to recreate their pleasing proportions. To Jefferson, the best manifestations of these timeless rules of taste were the great edifices of classical antiquity that had been recorded and codified in those books. Jefferson learned to recognize and appreciate the beauty in architecture that derived from simplicity, regularity, and proportion rather than from arbitrarily applied ornament, and he sought to instill this sensibility in his fellow countrymen by providing architectural models.

CENTRAL COLLEGE

A University bill, although under consideration in February 1817, failed to pass the Senate. Jefferson, in the meantime, turned with singleness of purpose to his plans for the first meeting of the Visitors of the Central College. He proceeded on the assumption that he would sway the Legislature to name Charlottesville as the location for a state university; designing three-dimensional textbooks demonstrating the correct use of the classical orders of architecture was also on his agenda.

With the general architectural arrangement of the buildings already designed (the plan of 1814), the first task was to select a site. On April 8, 1817, the journey from concept to reality began when Jefferson and two other Visitors selected a site along Three Notched Road, a major route between Richmond and the west. The land belonged to John Perry but had once belonged to one of the Visitors, President James Monroe. It was "a poor old turned out field" about one mile west of the town of Charlottesville and approximately three miles west of Jefferson's Monticello.[33] Bordered on the north by Three Notched Road and on the south by Wheeler's Road (the present-day University Avenue

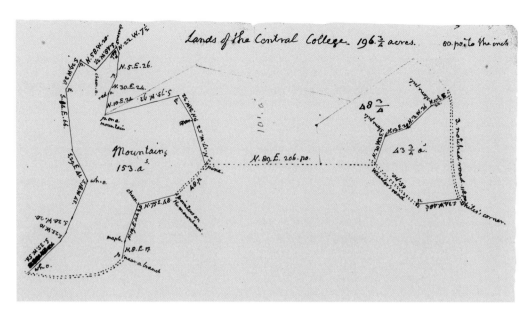

5. Thomas Jefferson. *Lands of the Central College*, c. 1819. Ink on paper, 9¾ x 8 (sheet). N-554, item 2. Jefferson Papers.

and Jefferson Park Avenue, respectively), it consisted of a narrow ridge declining gently in elevation from Three Notched Road southward for several hundred feet and then declining rather more sharply as it neared Wheeler's Road (fig. 5). Such irregular topography conflicted with Jefferson's idealized plan for a large, open, and flat site.

A few days later, although the entire Board of Visitors had not yet examined and approved the site, Jefferson sent a letter to James Dinsmore, one of his former master builders at Monticello. He requested that Dinsmore and John Neilson, who had also worked at Monticello, become builders for the college, and he summed up the situation:

We are about to establish a College near Charlottesville on the lands formerly Col.º Monroe's, a mile above the town. we do not propose to erect a single grand building, but to form a square of perhaps 200 yards, and to arrange around that pavilions of about 24. by 36. f. [feet] one for every professorship & his school. they are to be of various forms, models of chaste architecture, as examples for the school of architecture to be formed on. we shall build one only in the latter end of this year, and go

on with the others year after year, as our funds increase. indeed we believe that our establishment will draw to it the great state university which is to be located at the next meeting of the legislature.[34]

Among the subjects discussed at the first full-scale Board of Visitors meeting on May 5, 1817, was the location and construction of the first pavilion. Jefferson presented his University Plan, and the Visitors voted to build a pavilion based on this scheme, instructing the Proctor,

so soon as the funds are at his command, to agree with proper workmen for the building of one, of stone or brick below ground, and of brick above, of substantial work, of regular architecture, well executed and to be completed, if possible, during the ensuing summer and winter; that the lot for the said pavilions be delineated on the ground of the breadth of ___ feet, with two parallel sides of indefinite length.[35]

The blank left for the width of the Lawn indicates that Jefferson had still not determined what the site restrictions were going to be in relation to his original concept.

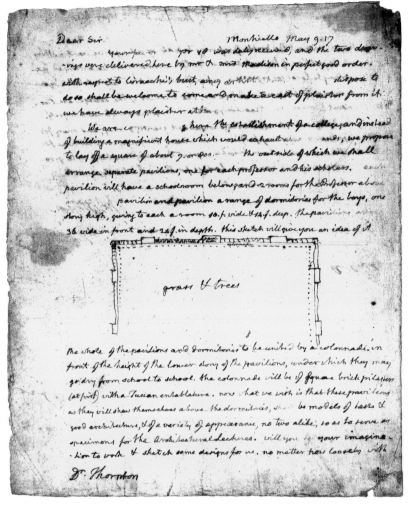

6. Thomas Jefferson. Letter to William Thornton, May 9, 1817, including sketch of the Lawn. Ink on laid paper, 10¼ x 8½. N-300. Jefferson Papers.

Shortly after the May 1817 Board meeting, Jefferson initiated correspondence first with Dr. William Thornton, then Benjamin Henry Latrobe, concerning the design of the college. He sketched the ground plan for Thornton and requested that Thornton make some suggestions for the pavilions. Thornton had won the competition for the United States Capitol and had designed other buildings in Washington.

By 1817 Jefferson was an accomplished designer and builder with an impressive body of work behind him, including his own Monticello estate, the Virginia State Capitol, designs (though not built) for the United States Capitol and President's House, his Poplar Forest plantation, and numerous courthouses and private homes. Jefferson, who had once been described as "an excellent architect out of books," normally sought design inspiration from the many architectural treatises that lined the shelves of his library.[36] However, in 1815 he had sold his books, including those on architecture, to the Library of Congress to replace those burned by British troops during the War of 1812. When it was decided at the May 5, 1817, Board of Visitors meeting to build the first pavilion that year, Jefferson's instinctive habit of turning to his books for ideas was thwarted by the empty walls of his library. He was thus forced to seek design assistance from an outside source, Thornton. As late as November 1817, Jefferson still had not replaced his copy of Palladio and had to ask James Madison to loan him his personal copy.[37]

At the time of the May 1817 Board of Visitors meeting, Jefferson may have received a replacement copy of another book sold in 1815 that would be instrumental to his classical pavilion designs: Roland Fréart de Chambray and Charles Errard's *Parallèle de l'Architecture Antique avec la Moderne* (Paris, 1766), which as the title suggests contained comparative drawings of classical orders from both ancient buildings and modern architectural writers, among them Palladio.[38] Jefferson had made use of this book when specifying the Tuscan, Doric, Ionic, and Corinthian entablatures on the interior of Monticello, as pencil notations on his surviving original copy at the Library of Congress demonstrate. This concise and comprehensive book, however, illustrated only partial elevations of the orders and did not show examples of their use. Thus, even if Jefferson had at his disposal these detailed illustrations of several choice examples of the classical orders, he lacked a design source that would have given him ideas for arranging them in different forms on the facades of the pavilions.

In his letter to Thornton on May 9 (fig. 6), Jefferson ignored the obvious topographic restrictions of the site:

we propose to lay off a square of about 7. or 800 [feet] the outside of which we shall arrange separate pavilions, one for each professor and his scholars. each pavilion will have a schoolroom below and 2 rooms for the Professor above and between pavilion and pavilion a range of dormitories for the boys, one story high.... this sketch will give you an idea of it. the whole of the pavilions and dormitories to be united by a colonnade in front of the height of the lower story of the pavilions, under which they may go dry from school to school. The colonnade will be of square brick pilasters (at first) with a Tuscan entablature. now what we wish is that these pavilions as they will shew [sic] themselves above the dormitories, [should] be models of taste and good architecture, & of a variety of appearance, no two alike, so as to serve as specimens for the architectural lectures. will you set your imagination to work & sketch some designs for us, no matter how loosely with the pen, without the trouble of referring to scale or rule; for we want nothing but the outline of the architecture, as the internal must be arranged according to local convenience.[39]

Jefferson received Thornton's reply on June 11, 1817, with a profusion of suggestions for the ground plan and buildings, as well as Thornton's own version of a four-tier system of public education. On a separate enclosure were two elevations for pavilions and their adjacent dormitories. Both of Thornton's pavilion facades employed the same motif of freestanding columns above an arcaded ground story (fig. 7).[40] He explained: "I have drawn a Pavilion for the Centre, with Corinthian Columns, & a Pediment." This more elaborate pavilion, Thornton suggested, would be the focus of the composition, the hierarchical center. He also recommended that pavilions be located at the corners of the square and that to initiate the Ionic order Jefferson need only "to convert the sketches already given." Thornton's single design

concept for the pavilions did not satisfy Jefferson's request for models with "a variety of appearance, no two alike," prompting him to write an almost identical request to architect Benjamin Henry Latrobe on June 12, the day after receiving Thornton's response.[41]

Latrobe wrote on June 17 that he had "derived important professional improvement from the entirely novel plan of an Academy suggested by you," and again on June 28 that he had "found so much pleasure in studying the plan of your College, that the drawings have grown into a larger bulk than can be conveniently sent by the Mail."[42] Latrobe's second letter did not reach Jefferson until July 15, and on the 16th he wrote to Latrobe requesting that he

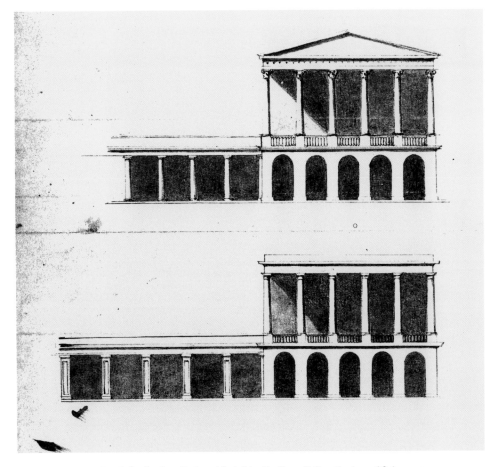

7. William Thornton. Facade Studies for a Doric and Corinthian Pavilion with Two Versions of Columns on the Connecting Colonnades. May or June 1817. Pricking, pencil, light-gray writing ink, India ink, watercolor on wove paper, 9½ x 7½ (sheet). N-303/352. Jefferson Papers.

send the plans as soon as possible because they were making bricks for the first pavilion, which had to be completed by fall. In this same letter Jefferson revealed for the first time that the sloping site would be terraced with a pavilion and twenty dormitories on each side of each terrace. Regarding the problem of finding competent workmen, Jefferson asked Latrobe if he could obtain a mason capable of executing a Doric base and capital, indicating that a Doric pavilion would be built first.[43]

On July 18, just two days after he wrote to Latrobe, Jefferson surveyed the site of the Academical Village and laid off the three terraces that were to become the Lawn. Faced with the necessity of a much narrower arrangement of pavilions and dormitories, he modified his 1814 conceptual ground plan by

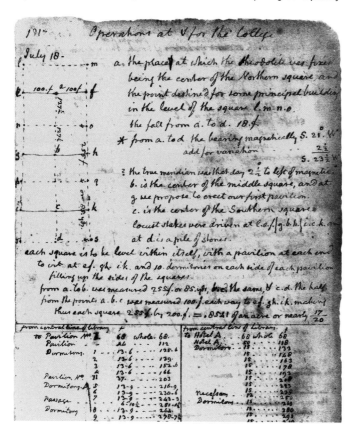

8. Thomas Jefferson, "Operations at and for the College," July 18, 1817. Detail from Specification Book, page 3, recto: iron-gall ink on paper, 8 x 4⅞. N-318. Jefferson Papers.

eliminating the buildings along one side of the square and moving the remaining two parallel rows closer together. Topographically, the space between the parallel rows of buildings now became virtually flat from east to west and, following the natural slope of the ridge, declined some eighteen feet from north to south. Jefferson divided this 200-foot-wide strip of land into three flat terraces, each 255 feet long, which would accommodate twenty dormitories, each ten feet wide, and a thirty-four-foot-wide pavilion, the same dimensions shown on his 1814 University Plan. He sketched a diagram of the Lawn in his specification book for the college (fig. 8), and identified point "g" (the center of the west side of the middle terrace) as the location for the first pavilion. Jefferson used letters to indicate other pavilions, describing point "a" in the center of the northern terrace as the future site for "some principal building," indicating that he already realized that a more substantial structure would be appropriate. Also, he did not locate any pavilions at the corners of the Lawn, as suggested by Thornton; instead his scheme called for dormitories extending north of the two northern pavilions.[44] And he indicated the "principle building" standing alone, without any connection to the dormitories and pavilions.

On July 19, 1817, the day after making the survey, Jefferson wrote to General Cocke, informing him that "our squares are laid off, the brickyard begun, and the levilling [sic] will be begun in the course of the week." He informed Cocke that subscriptions were coming in faster than anticipated and that they needed a Board of Visitors meeting right away to take care of pressing matters.[45] During a meeting in July at Madison's home, Montpelier, the Visitors, obviously strongly influenced by Thornton's drawings, approved a design for the first pavilion (fig. 9).[46]

Finally, on August 2, 1817, Jefferson received the first indication from Latrobe of what his eagerly anticipated pavilion designs might look like. In rough sketches, Latrobe suggested pavilions with giant-order porticoes—large columns running through both stories of the pavilion rather than the two single-story orders of Thornton—and a large domed building in the cen-

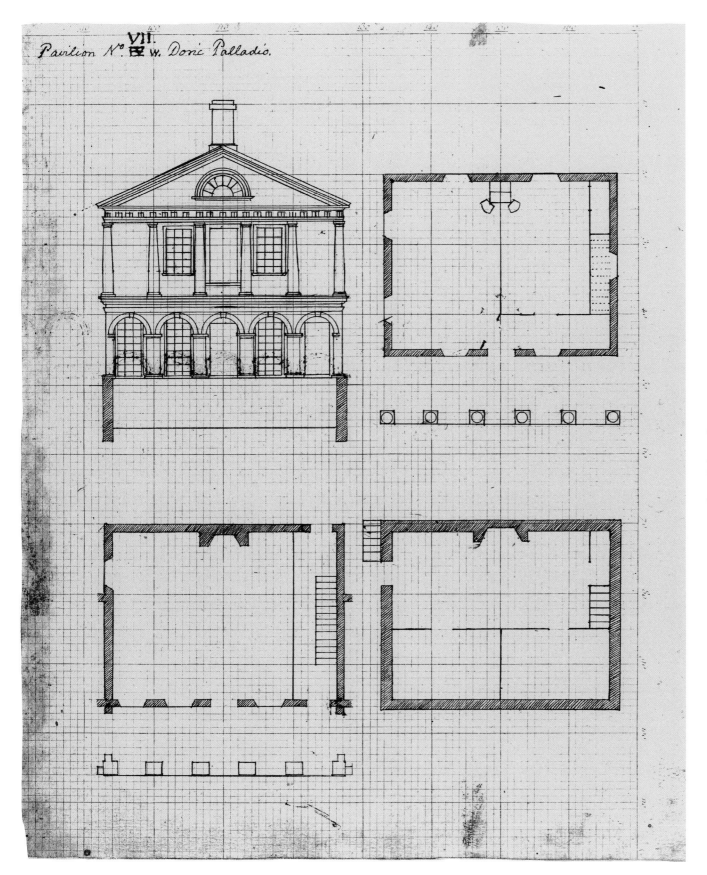

Pavilion Nº VII. W. Doric Palladio.

9. Thomas Jefferson. Study for Pavilion VII, July 1817. Pricking, scoring, iron-gall ink on laid paper engraved with coordinate lines, 11¾ x 10⅝. N-311. Jefferson Papers.

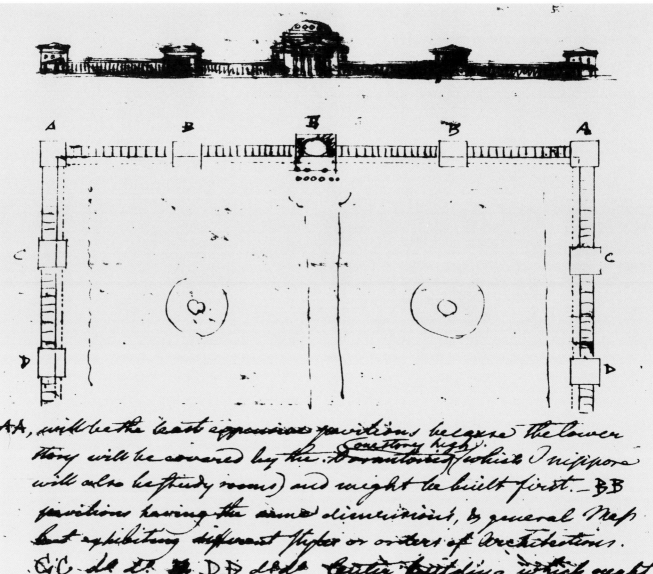

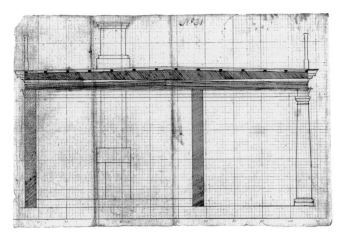

11. Thomas Jefferson. Study for Section of Dormitory and Colonnade, July 1817. Pricking, scoring, iron-gall ink on laid paper engraved with coordinate lines, 7¼ x 11¼. N-367. Jefferson Papers.

ter that would serve as a focal point (fig. 10). The ground plan and elevation were both based on Jefferson's original large, open-square concept. However, in responding to Jefferson's subsequent site description, Latrobe suggested that the plan could be adapted to a sloping site by detaching the east and west rows from the upper row.[47]

Jefferson responded to Latrobe's letter the next day, August 3, 1817, indicating that he had executed his design for the dormitories, and that they would construct a colonnade similar to the wings of the White House in Washington. He also explained to Latrobe that all of the pavilions at this point would be based on Thornton's two-story motif: "the whole basement story with the dormitories will be Tuscan with arches at the pavilions and columns in front of the dormitories[.] the pavilion now begun is to be a regular Doric above with a portico ... supported by the arches below and a pediment of the

whole breadth of the front. The columns 16 I.[inch] diam. the dormitories will be covered flat as the offices of the President's house at Washington...." (figs. 11, 12).[48]

Jefferson included a sketch showing the new arrangement of buildings necessitated by the topography. Having rethought the location of the "principle building," he moved it from the center of the northern terrace to the periphery. He wrote that "we leave open the [northern] end ... that if the state should establish there the University they contemplate, they may fill it up with something of the grand kind" (fig. 13). This point on the ground plan became the position of the Latrobe-inspired Rotunda, and in fact Jefferson did not wait for the official adoption of Central College as the state university before he began making plans to place Latrobe's domed central-building design at the head of the Lawn.[49]

The cornerstone of the first pavilion (subsequently named Pavilion VII) was laid with due ceremony on October 6, 1817. Jefferson had combined Thornton's suggestions with his own and based its order on the Doric of Palladio. The long-awaited sheet of Latrobe drawings finally arrived on October 8. Jefferson acknowledged the beautiful drawings in a letter four days later, informing Latrobe that they would select two of his fronts for their Ionic and Corinthian pavilions, which would be built the next season. After receiving Latrobe's varied pavilion designs, Jefferson had abandoned the Thornton scheme for the remaining pavilions on the Lawn.[50]

The brick walls were well underway on Pavilion VII when Jefferson's chief legislative advocate and fellow Visitor, Joseph C. Cabell, asked him to

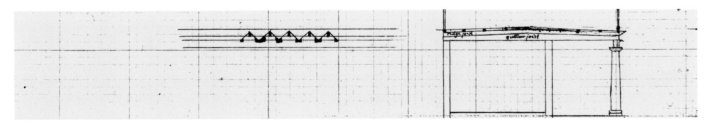

12. Thomas Jefferson. Study of Dormitory, July 1817. Ink on laid paper engraved with coordinate lines, 1⅝ x 9¾. N-406. Coolidge Collection, Massachusetts Historical Society, Boston.

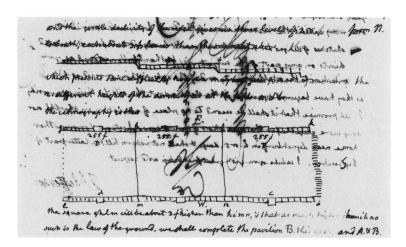

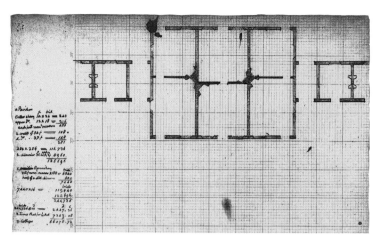

13. Thomas Jefferson. Ground Plan, included in letter to Benjamin Henry Latrobe, August 3, 1817. Ink on paper. Thomas Jefferson Papers, Library of Congress, Washington, D.C.

14. Thomas Jefferson. College Plan: Study for the Plan of Pavilion and Dormitory Units, October 24, 1817. Ink and pencil on engraved coordinate paper, 10⅛ x 13⅛ (sheet). N-299. Coolidge Collection, Massachusetts Historical Society, Boston.

draft another education bill, which Jefferson forwarded on October 24, 1817. Similar to his 1778 proposal, the draft bill advocated elementary schools, district colleges, and a university, and included a separate provision for converting the subscriptions and buildings of Central College if the Legislature were to choose it as the site of the university. The section calling for nine district colleges contained a written description of the building facilities, which he proposed have dormitories either in or adjacent to the school building. Because he was attempting to conform to the financial means of the Literary Fund, he drew a plan and calculated the cost to show that these projects would meet the budget. Jefferson had based this "College Plan" on the University Plan of 1814, but he omitted connecting covered passageways and included faculty residences and teaching rooms of one story in height without porticos (fig. 14).[51]

In spite of his "Utopian dream" of public education for all Virginians, Jefferson told George Ticknor shortly after submitting this bill that his hopes were "kept in check by the ordinary character of our state legislatures, the members of which do not generally possess information enough to perceive the important truths, that knowledge is power, that knowledge is safety, and that knowledge is happiness."[52] His skepticism was well-founded, as the struggle had already been going on for thirty-nine years.

In the meantime, Jefferson had turned to the question of how to pro-

ceed with the limited funding at hand. He submitted to the Board of Visitors a cost estimate for four pavilions (including Pavilion VII, then under construction), eighty dormitories, and two boarding houses. This was the first time he mentioned boarding houses for "dieting" the students.[53] Professorships were grouped into four categories, one each for languages, physiology, mathematics, and philosophy. Very clearly, Jefferson and the Board intended to install a university curriculum for Central College but on a limited scale.[54]

On February 19, 1818, the next step in Jefferson's dream was realized when the State Senate finally voted to establish a university and provided for a Commission to meet the following August at Rockfish Gap, Virginia, to recommend the site.[55] Named a commissioner, Jefferson campaigned to assure that Central College would become the University of Virginia. By May 1818 he had begun to prepare a report for consideration by the Commission, and on May 19, in his last known letter to Latrobe, he reported that they expected the Legislature would choose the site of Central College as the university, and that "this will call, in the first instance for about 16 pavilions, with an appendix of 20 dormitories each…. we propose 10 professors … and for each two professorships we must erect an hotel [dining hall] of the same good architecture." He informed Latrobe that he would use several of his suggestions for pavilion facades and that his domed structure would be "the Center of the ground."[56]

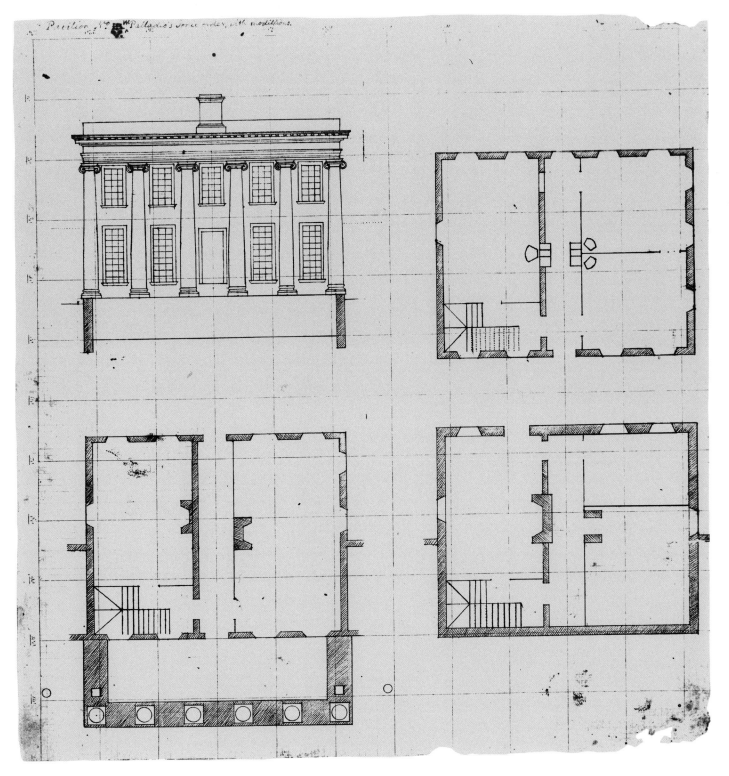

Pavilion No. Palladio's Ionic order, with modillions.

15. Thomas Jefferson. Study for Pavilion V, c.1818. Pricking, scoring, iron-gall ink on laid paper engraved with coordinate lines, 12¼ x 11½. N-356. Jefferson Papers.

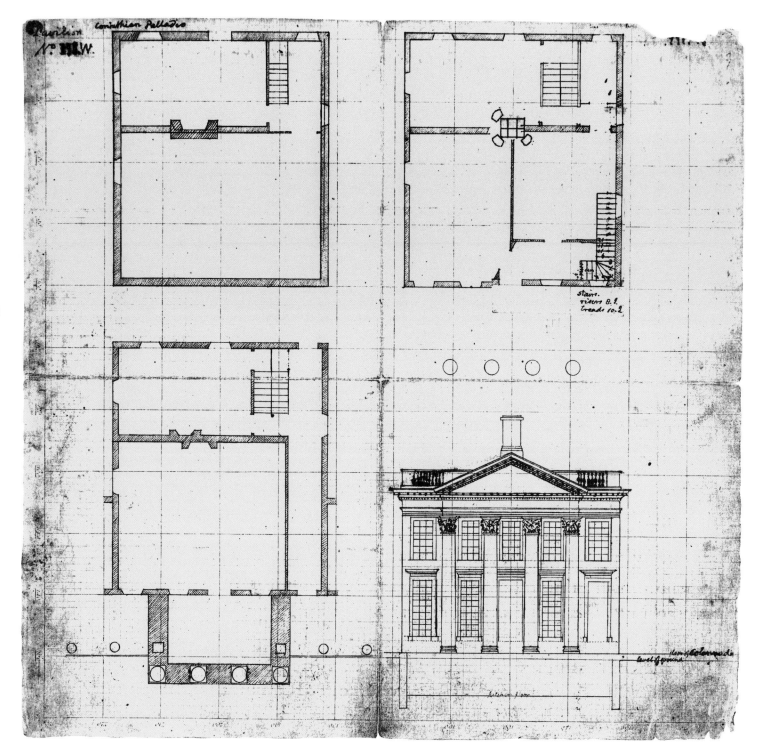

16. Thomas Jefferson. Study for Pavilion III, c. 1818. Pricking, scoring, iron-gall ink on laid paper engraved with coordinate lines, 11½ x 12⅛. N-316. Jefferson Papers.

The Visitors of the Central College had decided in October to build dormitories adjacent to the pavilion already begun and to build two more pavilions in 1818, along with their dormitories, but they had also decided to level the terraces before starting any more construction (fig. 15).[57] This grading process had been underway quite some time when Dinsmore arrived at Monticello on May 26, 1818, to discuss with Jefferson arrangements for construction of the second pavilion (Pavilion III on the West Lawn).[58] Jefferson had chosen one of the giant-order designs from Latrobe's sheet of drawings, specifically his "Palladian Corinthian, being the left hand figure of the upper row ... in which we permit no alteration but the substitution of a flat, for the pyramidal roof, which seen over the pediment, has not, we think, a pleasing effect" (fig. 16).[59]

On the interior of Pavilion III, Jefferson used the same entablature in the professor's upstairs parlor as in the entrance hall at Monticello.[60] Similarly a semi-circular arched doorway in the pavilion hallway echoed the library at Monticello (fig. 17). Dinsmore, the builder of Pavilion III, had executed the joinery at Monticello, so he was thoroughly familiar with Jefferson's favorite design motifs. The interior designs of subsequent pavilions bore the personal marks of their different craftsmen.

Site limitations posed a problem with the location of Pavilion III, since the level ground for the middle terrace north of Pavilion VII extended only ninety-three feet. This reduced the middle terrace to only about 220 feet in overall length, not the 255 feet Jefferson had laid out the year before. He drew a new ground plan based on Dinsmore's measurements and placed Pavilion III at the center of what would now be a slightly larger northern terrace; and he drew only nine dormitories on each side of Pavilion VII to fill up the middle terrace. Jefferson drew the Lawn at the prescribed 200-foot width and indicated with a circle the "principal building" centered on the north end of the Lawn. The seventy-seven-foot diameter of this structure reveals that he had formulated, at least in part, his plans for the future Rotunda, which had been inspired by Latrobe's drawing. Intending to finish both pavilions and their

17. Pavilion III: arched doorway in entry hallway separating living quarters from classroom. (Photograph by Bill Sublette.)

dormitories by the fall, workmen broke ground on Pavilion III and the nine dormitories south of Pavilion VII in June 1818.[61]

Jefferson continued his campaign for a university in Charlottesville and invited fellow commissioners L.W. Tazewell, Judge Roane, and James Madison to visit Monticello two days before the Rockfish Gap meeting in August 1818 in order to coordinate strategy.[62] Having expressed confidence to Tazewell that two-thirds of the commissioners would be in favor of Charlot-

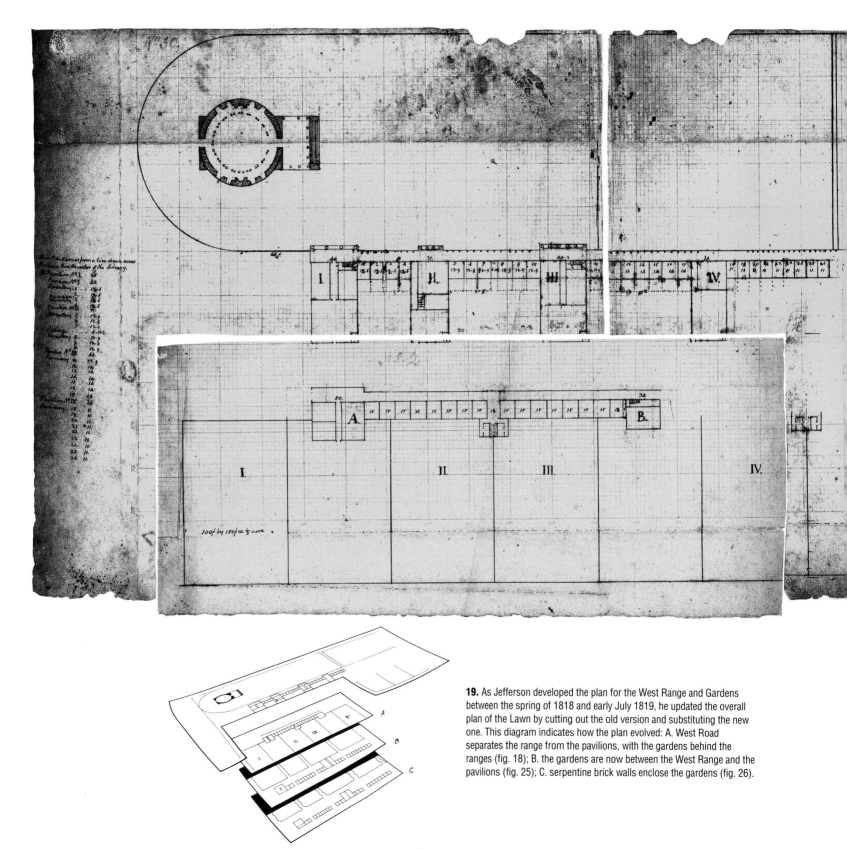

19. As Jefferson developed the plan for the West Range and Gardens between the spring of 1818 and early July 1819, he updated the overall plan of the Lawn by cutting out the old version and substituting the new one. This diagram indicates how the plan evolved: A. West Road separates the range from the pavilions, with the gardens behind the ranges (fig. 18); B. the gardens are now between the West Range and the pavilions (fig. 25); C. serpentine brick walls enclose the gardens (fig. 26).

from the line thro' the center of the library
to Hotel A 60
Hotel A 74
Dormitory 10
alley 15
16
12·7
12·7
12·7
12·7
14·7
12·7
alley 12
Dormitory 12
12
Hotel B 50
dormitory 12
12
13
alley 13
Dormitory 14
14·8
14·8
14·8
14·8
14·8
14·8
14·8
alley

18. Thomas Jefferson. Study for Lawn with Pavilions and Rotunda, 12¾ x 27¼, N-366. Inset: study for West Range of Dormitories and Gardens, 6¼ x 14¾, N-306. Both executed between March 3 and March 29, 1819; pricking, scoring, iron-gall ink on laid paper engraved with coordinate lines. Jefferson Papers.

tesville, his proposals were approved at the August meeting. The Rockfish Gap Commission report went to the Assembly in the late fall of 1818, and on January 25, 1819, a charter establishing the University of Virginia was passed, naming Charlottesville and the buildings begun at Central College as the site.[63]

THE UNIVERSITY OF VIRGINIA

Jefferson finally had his dream within his grasp. For forty years, he had championed a university in Virginia where all the useful sciences would be taught in their highest degree. He began to expand the Central College facilities to accommodate the new University of Virginia.

Jefferson immediately set about opening a classical academy in Charlottesville; under the tutelage of a Mr. Stack from Philadelphia, students would be prepared to enter the University.[64] Because he hoped to open the University on a limited scale by the following year, his schedule demanded a vigorous building program, as well. Advertisements for workmen were placed in Richmond and as far away as Philadelphia. On March 3, 1819, Arthur S. Brockenbrough, who had been hired as Proctor to direct the building campaign, arrived, relieving from Jefferson's shoulders "a burthen [*sic*] too much for them."[65]

That life had become a "burthen" is not surprising. Before the Visitors' meeting on March 29, 1819, Jefferson prepared all of the specifications and plans for that year's buildings, and he more than doubled the size of the project (figs. 18, 19). In the revised ground plan, rather than extend the Lawn southward, as earlier schemes had suggested, he placed additional dormitories and the hotels behind the pavilions and dormitories (now somewhat larger and greatly reduced in number) that bordered the West Lawn, thus creating more parallel rows of buildings detached from the central core. Although he omitted the fifth pavilion (IX) from this scheme, Jefferson numbered its site as "V" and had already executed its design (fig. 20).[66]

In the March 1819 ground plan, the design of the Rotunda came more

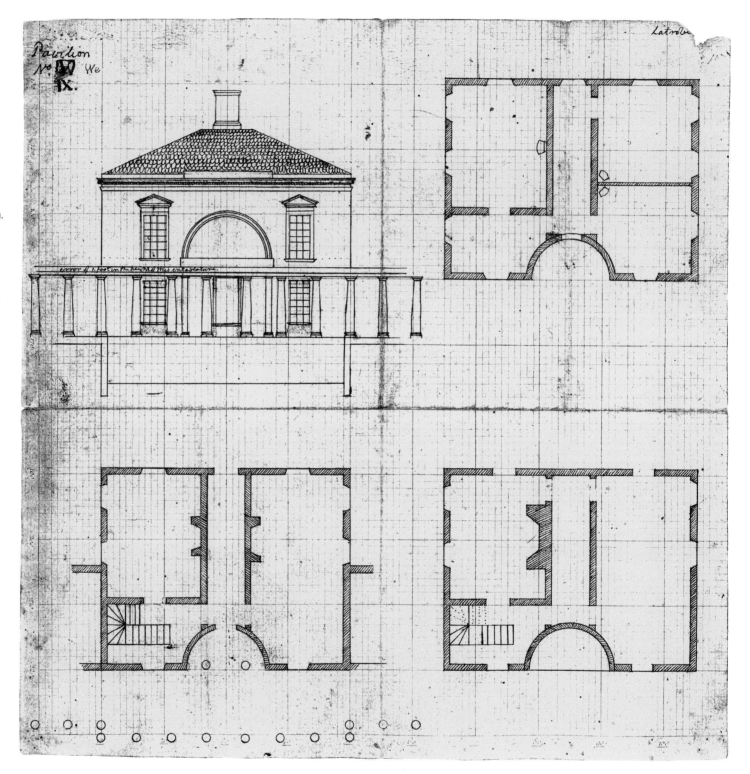

20. Thomas Jefferson. Study for Pavilion IX, c. March 29, 1819. Pricking, scoring, iron-gall ink on laid paper engraved with coordinate lines, 11⅛ x 11⅛. N-357. Jefferson Papers.

into focus (fig. 21). Jefferson showed a coupled-column configuration, and the other drawings were probably in hand. He had originally intended to use twenty Corinthian columns for the Rotunda's Dome Room, and the erasures he made when changing to forty coupled columns remain on the plan.[67] This alteration also called for a change in the height of the galleries to accommodate the shorter height of the columns; erasure marks around the galleries on the section drawing indicate their previous heights (fig. 22). The columns shown in this section are Corinthian, and because the height of the columns correspond to Palladio's proportions for the Corinthian order and not the Composite, as executed, the coupled Corinthian columns were apparently an intermediate design choice.

On the back of his drawing Jefferson acknowledged that he had based the design for the Rotunda on the Pantheon in Rome. He wrote that its diameter is "77. feet, being ½ that of the Pantheon, consequently ¼ it's [*sic*] area, & ⅛ it's volume." However, the Rotunda was not a one-half-scale reproduction of the Pantheon as illustrated in Leoni's Palladio (figs. 23, 24). Even the most cursory comparison of the two facades reveals numerous differences, the most obvious being that the Pantheon has an octastyle portico while the portico fronting Jefferson's Rotunda is only six columns wide. Clearly there is a missing link between the Rotunda and the Pantheon. Jefferson's design derives not only from a Latrobe concept, but also from a now-missing Latrobe drawing. Jefferson had identified Latrobe twice by name on the Rotunda drawings: in the upper right-hand corner of the elevation he inscribed "Latrobe No. [illegible]," referring to Latrobe's numbered drawing, but it was subsequently crossed out; secondly, the specifications on the back of the Rotunda floor plan (fig. 21) now read, "Rotunda, reduced to the proportions of the Pantheon and accommodated to the purposes of a Library for the University," but close inspection reveals the erasure of "Latrobe's Rotunda, reduced to the proportions of the Pantheon...." Jefferson himself might have erased it, feeling that his reworking of the design sufficiently made it his own, but clearly Latrobe's influence on the

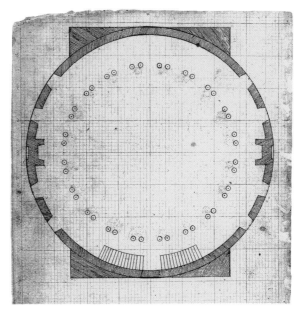

21. Thomas Jefferson. Plan for the Dome Room of the Rotunda (Library), begun 1818, completed by March 29, 1819. Pricking, scoring, iron-gall ink, pencil on laid paper engraved with coordinate lines, 12¼ x 8⅝ (sheet). N-331. Jefferson Papers.

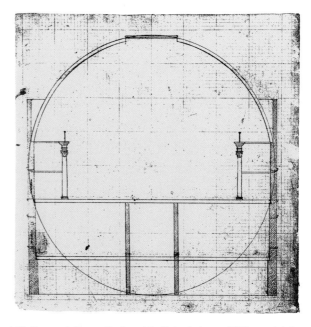

22. Thomas Jefferson. Section of the Rotunda, begun 1818, completed by March 29, 1819. Pricking, iron-gall ink on laid paper engraved with coordinate lines, 8¾ x 8¾. N-329. Jefferson Papers. (See fig. 23.)

23. Thomas Jefferson. South Elevation of the Rotunda, begun 1818, completed by March 29, 1819. Pricking, scoring, iron-gall ink, pencil on laid paper engraved with coordinate lines, 8¾ x 8¾. N-328. Jefferson Papers. This drawing was once on a single sheet, on the right, with the Rotunda section drawing, fig. 22, on the left.

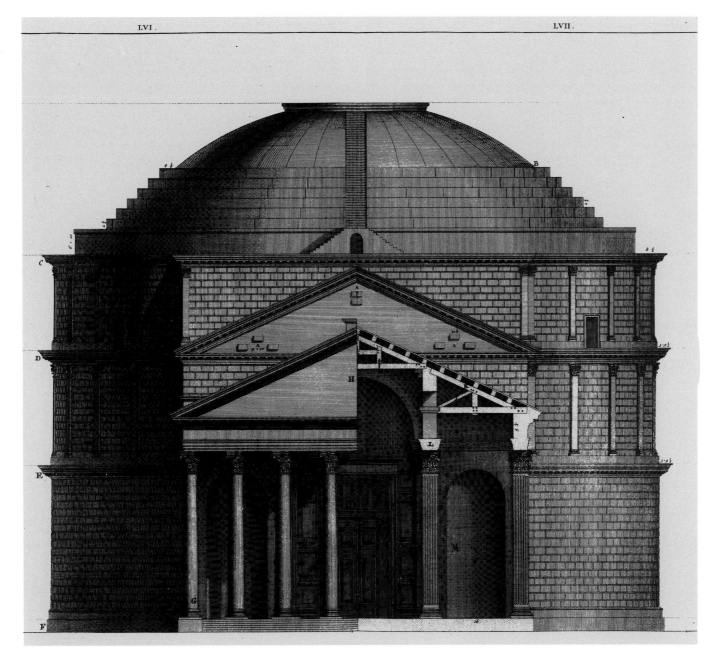

24. Andrea Palladio. "Half of the fore-front" and "Half of the front under the Portico," Plates LVI and LVII from Book IV, Chapter 20 ("Of the Pantheon, now call'd the Rotonda"), Giacomo Leoni. *Architecture of A. Palladio: In Four Books*, 3rd edition (London, 1742). Special Collections, Rare Books Division.

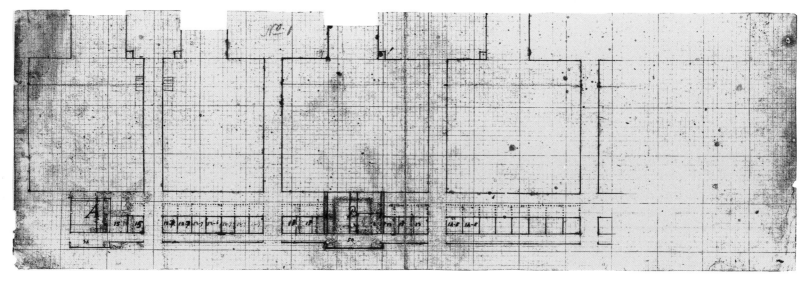

25. Thomas Jefferson. Ground Plan for West Range with Gardens (second version of March 1819 ground plan, see fig. 19), revised April 1819. Ink on laid paper engraved with coordinate lines, 5¼ x 16¾. N-305. Jefferson Papers. This drawing, showing gardens between the professors' pavilions and the range of hotels and dormitories, was substituted in the overall plan of the Lawn for the first plan of the West Range, N-306, shown in fig. 19, ostensibly to save time and paper.

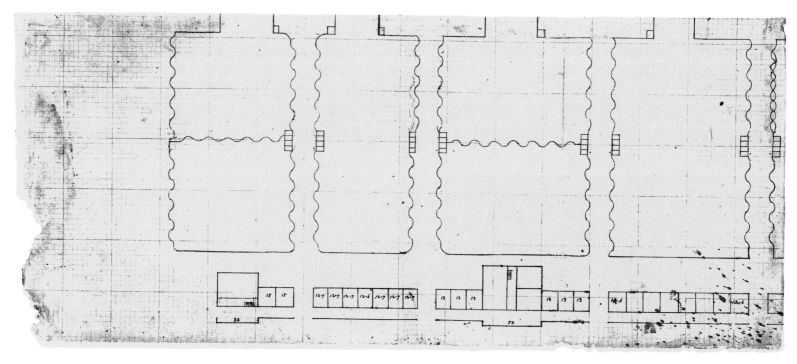

26. Thomas Jefferson. Ground Plan for West Range with Gardens (third version of March 1819 ground plan, see fig. 19), revised by July 8, 1819. Iron-gall ink on laid paper engraved with coordinate lines, 6½ x 15¾. N-369. Jefferson Papers. Again, a change in the garden plan was made by substituting this new drawing for the West Range in the first plan of the Lawn.

Rotunda's design was substantial. While the arrangement of the floor plans was worked out by Jefferson, and while he chose the architectural ornament from plates in the Leoni edition of Palladio, the overall exterior form of the building and its portico derives from Latrobe's missing design for the University's "principle building."[68]

With Jefferson's revised arrangement of buildings, each pavilion had only a small enclosed yard adjacent to the rear of the building; it was probably intended to hold horses and to store the professor's carriage. Additionally, all of the professors and hotel-keepers were to have access to individual garden plots located behind the outer row of hotels and dormitories. After the March 29, 1819, Board of Visitors meeting, at least one member, Joseph C. Cabell, expressed dissatisfaction with the latest arrangement of buildings and gardens, and he suggested that the gardens be relocated between the pavilions and hotels. At first Jefferson believed the proposed change was not possible because it would block access by horse and carriage to the rear of the pavilions. Still, he found Cabell's suggestion worth further study, and he returned to the drafting table to sketch out how it might be achieved.[69]

By April 15, 1819, Jefferson had cut the first version of the back range of hotels and dormitories from his latest ground-plan drawing and had inserted a new version in which the back range was facing away from the Lawn and was separated from it by large enclosed gardens (fig. 25). To solve the problem of access, he added a new feature to the ground plan: perpendicular alleys, or "cross streets of communication," running between the individual gardens and connecting the ranges of pavilions and hotels.[70] He reported to another member of the Board of Visitors, General James Breckenridge: "I think it a real improvement, and the greater, as by throwing the Hotels and additional dormitories on a back street, it forms in fact the commencement of a regular town, capable of being enlarged to any extent which future circumstances may call for."[71] A third version emerged by July 8, 1819, when Jefferson drew the famous serpentine walls for the gardens and inserted privies for the students. In this nearly final version, he moved the hotels even

further from the pavilions and included a dividing wall to provide garden space for each of the hotels (fig. 26). On an 1824 survey diagram, Jefferson named the roads in front of the hotels and ranges "East Street" and "West Street."

Jefferson did not work in a vacuum; he tested his ideas and sought advice from colleagues such as Thornton and Latrobe, as well as the Board of Visitors. Still, he usually had the final word when it came to architectural matters. Challenging Jefferson on any aspect of the project meant tiptoeing lightly. Joseph Cabell wrote to fellow Board member Cocke that when suggesting modifications, "We should move in concert or we shall perplex and disgust the old Sachem."[72] Suggestions that strayed very far from Jefferson's original conception did not fare well. Cocke, who shared with Jefferson the responsibility as a Committee of Superintendence, petitioned him to redesign the hotels and dormitories of the ranges. Jefferson's method of flat-roof construction concerned Cocke, and he suggested that, instead of copying the individual single-story, flat-roof dormitory rooms that faced the Lawn, they build multiple-story buildings with pitched roofs for a hotel-dormitory combi-

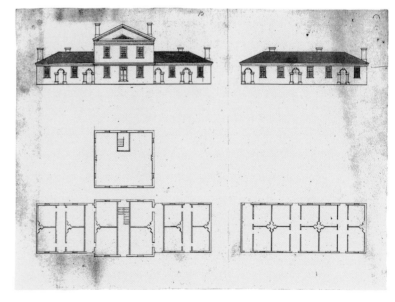

27. Attributed to General John H. Cocke. Studies for Dormitory. Pencil, India ink, gray wash on plain wove paper, 9 x 12⅜. N-375. Jefferson Papers.

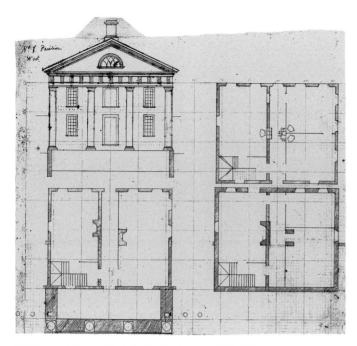

28. Thomas Jefferson. Study for Pavilion I, c. early 1819. Pricking, scoring, iron-gall ink on laid paper with engraved coordinate lines, 10⅝ x 11¾. N-355. Jefferson Papers.

nation on the back range (fig. 27).[73] Cocke's proposals were on a much grander scale than could be reconciled with Jefferson's more modest Academical Village concept, which revolved around individual dormitory rooms opening onto a covered walkway. Jefferson had sought to avoid all of the disadvantages associated with large buildings such as noise and the ease with which fire and infection could spread. He argued that

> the separation of the students in different and unconnected rooms, by two's and two's, seems a fundamental of the plan. it was adopted by the first visitors of the Central college … it was approved and reported by the Commissioners of Rockfish gap to the legislature…. not thinking therefore that the committee [of superintendence] was competent to this change, I concurred in suspending the building of any Hotel until the visitors should have an opportunity of considering the subject and instead of building one or two Hotels, as they directed, we concluded to

begin the Eastern range of pavilions, all agreeing that the ranges on each side of the lawn should be finished as begun.[74]

On June 5, 1819, Jefferson wrote to the Proctor, Arthur S. Brockenbrough, to inform him that

> as it is but lately concluded to commence the Eastern range of pavilions, & Dormitories I have not prepared the plans, nor shall I be at leisure to turn to that business till the week after the ensuing one. but those pavilions will vary so little from the dimensions last given, & those of No I. II. III. of the Western range that if the foundations are dug to that, the trimming them to what shall be the exact size of each will be trifling. [Fig. 28.]

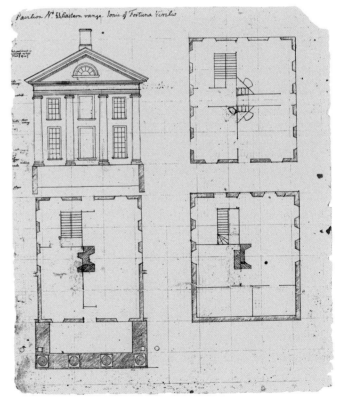

29. Thomas Jefferson. Study for Pavilion II, June 1819. Pricking, scoring, iron-gall ink on laid paper with engraved coordinate lines, 12 x 10. N-321. Jefferson Papers.

Three weeks later, the plans were complete and he was pressing for construction to begin (figs. 29–33).[75]

Although Jefferson designed the buildings and wrote exacting specifications for dimensions and the exterior orders to be used, he apparently did not create working drawings for the builders to follow. An 1819 advertisement for workmen that appeared in the *Richmond Enquirer* indicates that all workmen were required to furnish their own working "draughts" and that they had to be approved prior to beginning construction.[76] Upon approval, the plans remained in the possession of the builder and were probably worn out through use. This points to the fact that the workmen made important contributions to the different buildings, for they designed many of the interior details of entablatures, chimney-pieces, and other features.

Richard Ware, from Philadelphia, built Pavilions II and IV on the East Lawn. His impact can be seen in the pulvinated (convex) Ionic frieze and matching mantel in the upstairs parlor of Pavilion IV, which is the only known instance of its use in a design by Jefferson. The presence of this feature reveals that Ware used a pattern book different from Jefferson's Leoni Palladio, because Leoni had substituted a flat frieze for the convex version indicated by Palladio.

By October 1819, the hillside above Charlottesville teemed with workmen as seven pavilions and thirty-six dormitories were in various stages of completion. Slaves hired from local planters were still leveling the Grounds and digging out foundations. Over the years in excess of 200 individuals were involved in the construction. Workmen were lodged in the completed dormi-

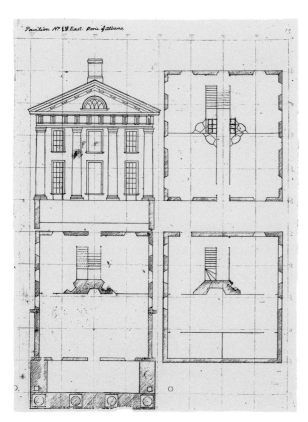

30. Thomas Jefferson. Study for Pavilion IV, June 1819. Pricking, scoring, iron-gall ink on laid paper with engraved coordinate lines, 12 x 8¾. N-322. Jefferson Papers.

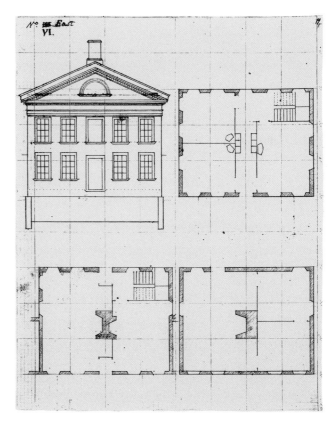

31. Thomas Jefferson. Study for Pavilion VI, June 1819. Pricking, scoring, iron-gall ink on laid paper with engraved coordinate lines, 11 x 8¾. N-324. Jefferson Papers.

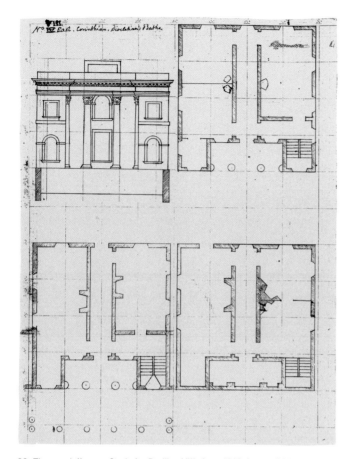

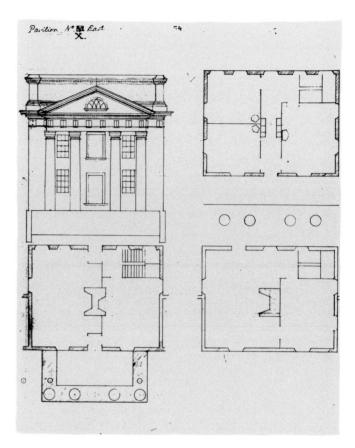

32. Thomas Jefferson. Study for Pavilion VIII, June 1819. Iron-gall ink on laid paper with engraved coordinate lines, 11½ x 8¾. N-325. Jefferson Papers.

33. Thomas Jefferson. Study for Pavilion X, June 1819. Pricking, iron-gall ink on laid paper with engraved coordinate lines, 11 x 9⅛. N-326. Jefferson Papers.

tories, including the basements, and elsewhere in boarding houses. Italian stonecutters, the Raggi brothers, were imported to carve the classical column capitals out of native stone, but that proved a disaster because the native stone could not be worked. Instead Carrara marble capitals were ordered from Italy.[77]

With construction on both sides of the Lawn now underway, the next step was to begin work on the hotels and dormitories of the ranges. At their meeting of April 3, 1820, the Board of Visitors agreed to finish the last three pavilions, the East Range of the hotels, then the West Range. For the East Range, Jefferson decided to reuse the single-story plan he had drawn for his first West Range study (fig. 34). However, the new arrangement of gardens and hotels created problems because not enough room existed to place the

large fifty-foot-wide hotel shown on his West Range plans at the north end of the East Range and still have room for dormitories adjacent to it. Jefferson was made aware of this and another problem in a letter from Arthur Brockenbrough: "I wish to see you also before we begin the foundations of the Hotels, as I find if we cut in the bank the depth of Hotel A we shall have a bank 7 feet high and then the cellar to dig out[.] in order to save some labor I propose advancing the building a few feet in the street & then throwing the street more to the East."[78] Jefferson responded with a new plan for a thirty-four-foot square hotel (now Hotel B) for the northern end of the East Range (fig. 35), thus allowing for the insertion of two dormitory rooms between the hotel and the alley, and he shifted the other two hotels (now D and F) to the second and third positions on the East Range. He also drew a new scheme for

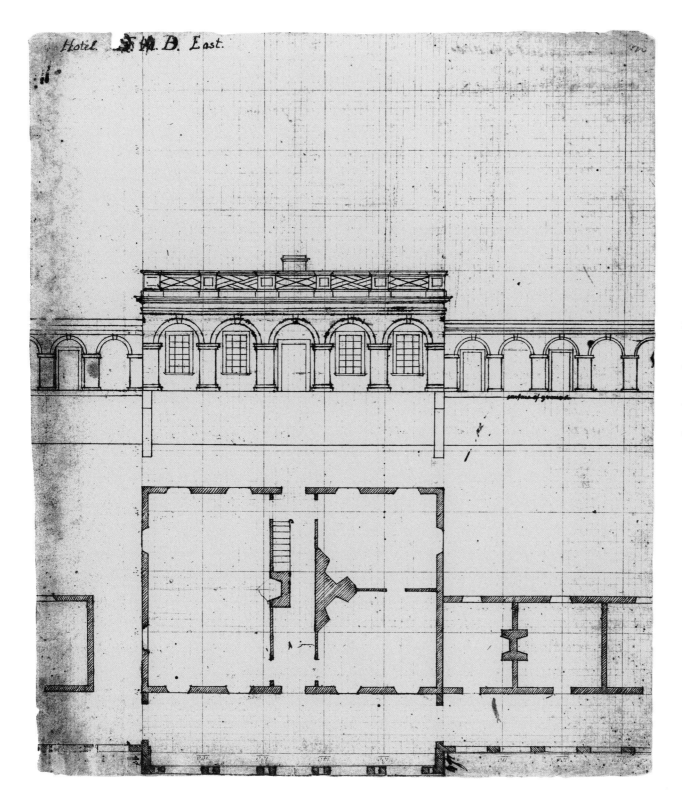

34. Thomas Jefferson. Study for Hotel D (originally Hotel B), completed by March 29, 1819. Pricking, iron-gall ink, pencil on laid paper with engraved coordinate lines, 12⅛ x 10¼. N-362. Jefferson Papers.

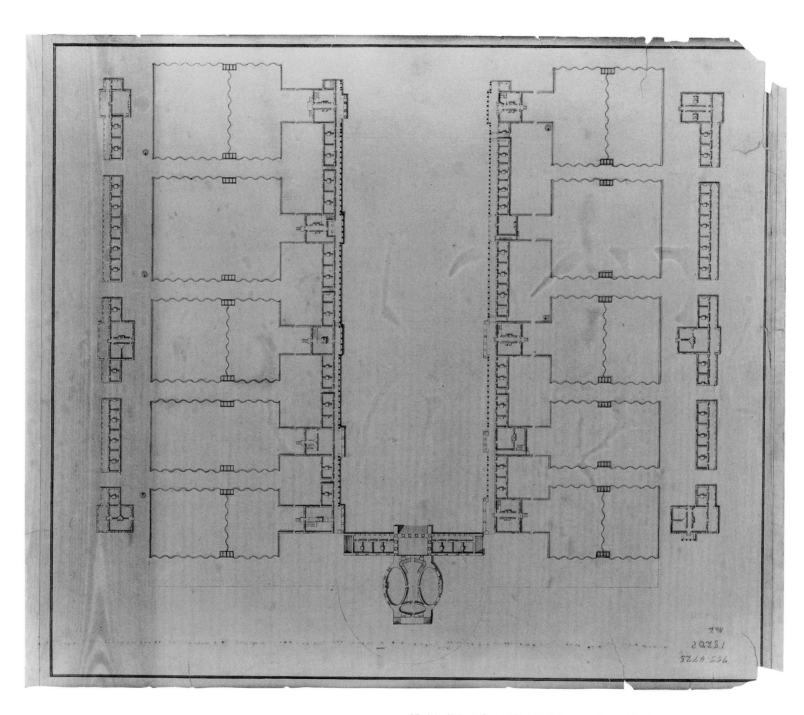

37. John Neilson. Ground Plan, study for engraving, c. March 1821. N-383. Ink on paper, 16¾ x 19½. N-383. Virginia State Library and Archives, Richmond.

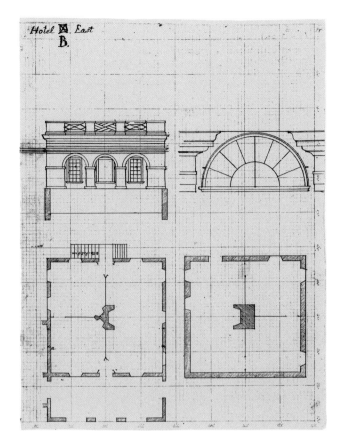

35. Thomas Jefferson. Study for Hotel B, c. May 1820. Pricking, iron-gall ink, pencil on laid paper with engraved coordinate lines, 11½ x 8¾. N-360. Jefferson Papers.

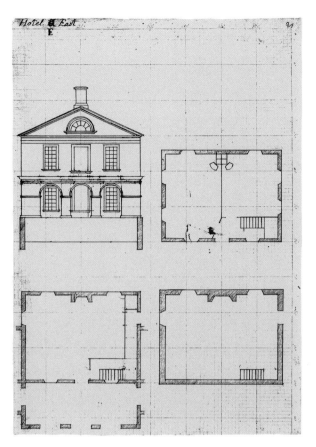

36. Thomas Jefferson. Study for Hotel F East, c. May 1820. Ink on laid paper with engraved coordinate lines, 11½ x 8¼. N-363. Jefferson Papers.

the two-story hotel (now F), changing its order from Ionic to Tuscan, and its arcade from five bays to three (fig. 36). All of the hotels after this were designed and built using the Tuscan order, and all six hotels contain at least one thirty-four-foot exterior wall, which had been the module for the University Plan of 1814.

Jefferson did not respond immediately to the request to move the street, because Brockenbrough wrote again on June 22 asking "the favor of you to permit us to advance the Eastern range of Hotels and dormitories about 17 feet—in order to save much labor in digging and removing earth." Jefferson eventually agreed, and the ground plan drawn by John Neilson in 1821 clearly shows the gardens on the east to be deeper than those on the west (fig. 37). It was one of many concessions Jefferson had to make in his constant at-

tempts to deal with an irregular site and maintain a sense of balance in the overall design. He obviously felt that he was making the right decisions, though, for he wrote in mid-1820 to John Wayles Eppes: "our university is now so far advanced as to be worth seeing. it exhibits already the appearance of a beautiful Academical Village, of the finest models of building and of classical architecture in the U.S. it begins to be much visited by strangers and admired by all, for the beauty, originality, and convenience of the plan."[79]

Plans were ready by the following March for the West Range, but none of them match any existing Jefferson drawing.[80] Several of Neilson's meticulously executed drawings in India ink and watercolor for pavilions and hotels were obviously final studies of Jefferson drawings and more nearly reflect the buildings as executed, but no drawings for Hotels A and C in Jefferson's hand

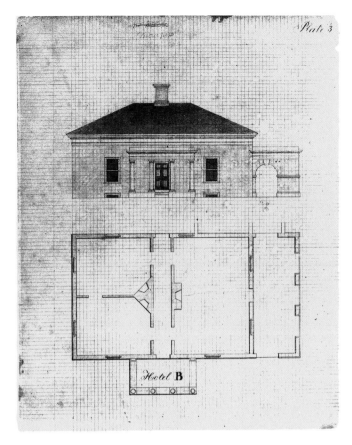

38. John Neilson. Study for Hotel A (labeled Hotel B), c. March 1821. Ink and watercolor on hand-ruled graph paper, 11½ x 9. N-339. Jefferson Papers.

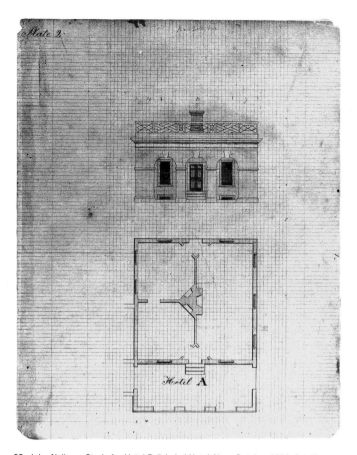

39. John Neilson. Study for Hotel B (labeled Hotel A), c. October 1820. Pricking, India ink, watercolor on hand-ruled graph paper, 11½ x 9. N-338. Jefferson Papers.

have been found. Also, Hotels A and C of the West Range are the only two buildings without some sort of documentation in Jefferson's specification book (fig. 38).[81] For Hotel C, Jefferson drew a plan, but he abandoned it before completion. He also drew one for the third in this line, and although it has the same exterior elevation it does not match Neilson's floor plan. Neilson's drawing for Hotel B is as built, with the entablature of the dormitories lower than that of the hotel (fig. 39).[82] Neilson's exact involvement in the design is unclear, but certainly he was following Jefferson's directions.

Neilson's ground plan of the entire University (fig. 37) was apparently the first Lawn study since Jefferson's 1814 plan. On each side of the Rotunda Neilson showed terraces ("terras"), or wings, with descending steps that gave access to eight rooms located underneath. For the April 1821 Board of

Visitors meeting, the Proctor, Arthur Brockenbrough, made an estimate of $42,000 to build the Rotunda, including the terraces and stone steps.[83] A second ground plan dating to about November 1821, with the University's name written across the bottom, shows sixteen rooms in the Rotunda's terrace (fig. 40).[84] The pavilions and hotels were numbered as they are today, and with the exception of the steps on the north side of the Rotunda they resemble the engraving done in 1822 by Peter Maverick from still another copy of the ground plan that has not been located (fig. 41). The back steps were in fact executed. Their existence was obscured by the Robert Mills addition of the 1850s.

William J. Coffee, a sculptor, artist, and maker of composition ornament, arrived at Monticello in December 1821. When he left around May 25,

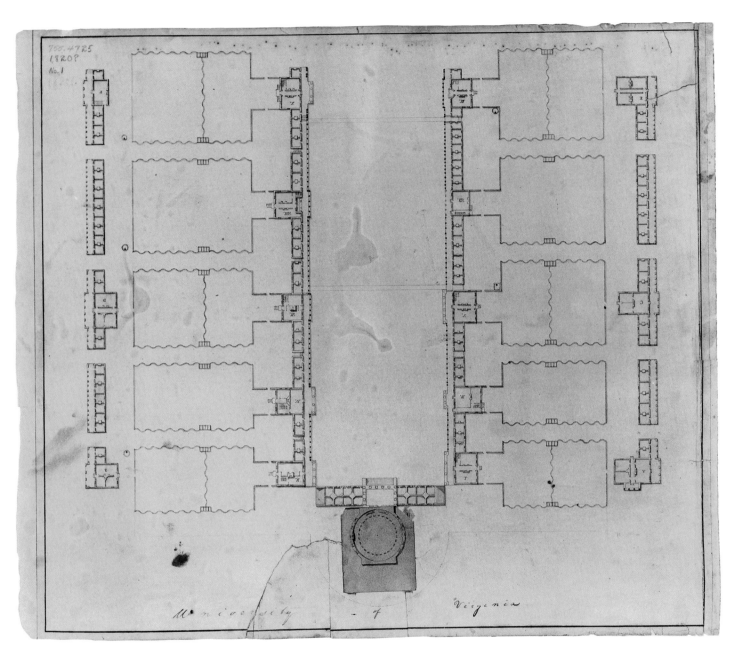

40. John Neilson. Ground Plan, study for engraving, c. November 1821. Ink on paper, 17 x 19½, with overlay of plan for Dome Room. N-382. Virginia State Library and Archives, Richmond.

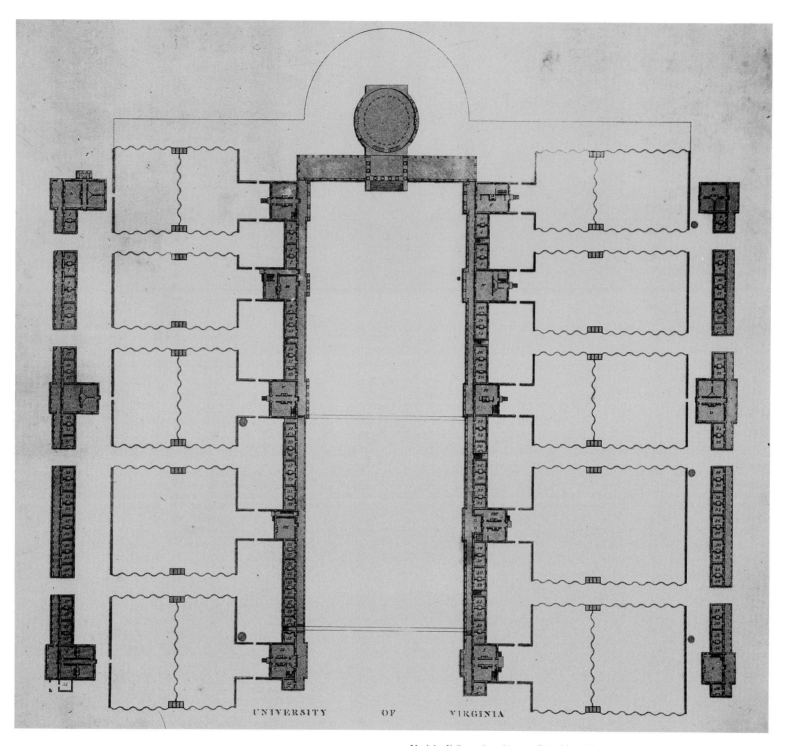

UNIVERSITY OF VIRGINIA

41. John Neilson, draughtsman; Peter Maverick, engraver.
University of Virginia (Ground Plan), 1822; revised edition
January-February 1825. Engraving, 19½ x 21 ⅞ (sheet). N-385.
Special Collections, Edwin M. Betts Collection.

1822, he carried with him the ground plan that was the basis for the Maverick engraving, as well as a detailed list of the ornament Jefferson had chosen for the interior and exterior entablatures of the pavilions. Work proceeded throughout 1822, so that by December construction was nearly complete, except for the Rotunda.[85]

Budget constraints had been a problem from the beginning. The 1818 Legislature provided an annuity of only $15,000 per year from the Literary Fund; when that amount was added to the $44,345 in private subscriptions pledged for Central College, the total did not allow for simultaneous construction, employment of professors, and purchase of equipment. Always short of money, the Board of Visitors took loans against annuities. The idea that they might open the University in 1820 was shelved so construction could be completed.[86] Jefferson, especially, was fearful of proceeding with the operation of the University. Concerned that the Rotunda would never be completed as he envisioned, he expressed his fear to Joseph C. Cabell in December 1822:

> The great object of our aim from the beginning, has been to make the establishment the most eminent in the United States, in order to draw to it the youth of every State, but especially of the south and west. We have proposed, therefore, to call to it characters of the first order of science from Europe, as well as our own country; and, not only by the salaries and the comforts of their situation, but by the distinguished scale of its structure and preparation, and the promise of future eminence which

> these would hold up, to induce them to commit their reputation to its future fortunes. Had we built a barn for a college, and log huts for accommodations, should we ever have had the assurance to propose to

42. Attributed to John Neilson (formerly attributed to Cornelia Jefferson Randolph). Study for Elevation of Rotunda and Pavilions IX (left) and X (right), February 1823. Pricking, pencil, India ink, iron-gall ink, and tinted washes on wove paper, 11 x 17½. N-354. Jefferson Papers.

> an European professor of that character to come to it? … to stop where we are is to abandon our high hopes, and become suitors to Yale and Harvard for their secondary characters.[87]

In February of 1823 the loan came through to build the Rotunda.

That same month, Neilson, who had contracted with Dinsmore to build the Rotunda, wrote to Cocke to tell him that he had drawn "an elevation of the Pantheon with the flank view of Pavillions [sic] No. 9 and 10 for Mrs. Cocke…. I have nearly finished all the drawings I intended and then I may take Holiday" (fig. 42).[88] Referring to his earlier versions of the ground plan, Neilson had drawn the terrace wings of the Rotunda as a continuous pedestal

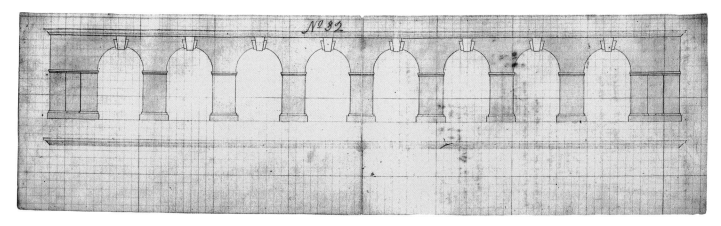

43. Attributed to John Neilson. Study for Gymnasium Arcades, March 1824. India ink, pencil, watercolor on hand-ruled graph paper, 4⅜ x 16⅛. N-368. Jefferson Papers.

to each side, and not connected to the colonnades of the East and West Lawns. The other drawings Neilson mentioned were probably working drawings.

In the spring of 1824, Jefferson, too ill to leave his bed and draw an elevation, directed Brockenbrough to extend an arcade along the front of the Rotunda terrace to the pavilions on either side, thus completing his original scheme for going dry from place to place.[89] Underneath would be a gymnasium where the young men could exercise in bad weather. Neilson executed the drawing (fig. 43). The 1825 version of the Maverick engraving incorporated this change (fig. 41).

Also in the spring of 1824, the Legislature gave the Visitors the financial means to put the University into operation as soon as practicable. With the Academical Village all but complete, Jefferson could now turn his attention to the long-awaited pleasure of filling it with students and the best professors in their respective sciences that he could find in all of Europe and America. At their meeting in April 1824, the Visitors appointed Francis Walker Gilmer as their agent to travel to Europe for the purpose of hiring professors and to purchase textbooks and apparatus necessary for the different professorships. They planned to open the following February.[90] Work continued on the Rotunda, and in November of 1824 the Library room was complete enough that the Marquis de Lafayette was entertained there at a dinner for four hundred.[91]

Finally, on March 7, 1825, the University opened its doors to approximately forty students and five professors. Dr. George Blatterman, a German who arrived from London in December, took the professorship of Modern Languages and was housed in Pavilion IV. Thomas Hewitt Key from Trinity College, Cambridge, became Professor of Mathematics and was assigned to Pavilion VIII. Dr. Robley Dunglison, a Scotsman living in London, was engaged for Anatomy and Medicine and got Pavilion X. Charles Bonnycastle, an Englishman, took the chair of Natural Philosophy and Pavilion VI. George Long, another fellow of Trinity College, Cambridge, came as Professor of Ancient Languages, moving into Pavilion V. Two Americans were also selected: John P. Emmet of New York came on April 8 as Professor of the School of Natural History and lived in Pavilion I; and George Tucker, a Congressman from Virginia, came in March as the Professor of Ethics and took possession of Pavilion IX.[92]

Students meeting in a classroom in the instructor's house may have been acceptable to some of the professors, but Dr. Dunglison found his combined living-working accommodation in Pavilion X to be an inadequate and, justifiably, inappropriate setting in which to conduct his classes on anatomy and the dissection of human cadavers. Jefferson, who by now was almost 82 years old, designed a separate facility, and the Board of Visitors agreed in March 1825 that upon receipt of the necessary funds "an anatomical theatre be built, as nearly as may be on the plan now exhibited to the board" (fig. 44).[93]

Jefferson's drawing for the Anatomical Theatre shows a geometric design consisting of a square circumscribing an octagonal amphitheater arrangement of rising seats. Perhaps one of the most important aspects of the Anatomical Theatre was its placement opposite Hotel A on West Street which would begin a new, fifth row of buildings. Jefferson even indicated a projecting arcade across its front. Sometime after the site for the Anatomical Theatre had been selected, an unknown draughtsman designed a fifth row of buildings with projecting arcades extending south from the Anatomical Theatre, but this scheme was never carried out (fig. 45).

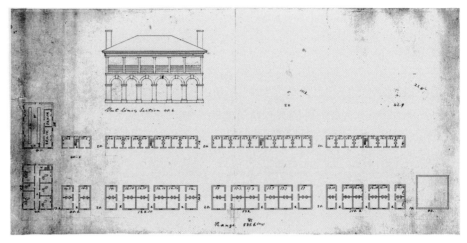

45. Unknown Renderer. Elevation and Plans of Dormitories for West Street, c. 1825. Ink on wove paper, 7¼ x 15½. N-377. Jefferson Papers.

1826 marked the ninth year of construction. Just days before Jefferson died on July 4, 1826, one student wrote, "The carpenters are progressing with the Rotunda and Anatomical theatre, and sometimes their racket disturbs my studying though I go on tolerable well (that is in my opinion)…. The number of students that have matriculated is 180, 12 of them have been expelled and suspended."[94]

Thomas Jefferson had forged the cornerstone of a nation in 1776. His ensuing quest to maintain the inalienable rights espoused in the Declaration of Independence was realized with the establishment of the University of Virginia as a grand seminary of learning to train future generations. The goal was to provide an educational program and facility second to none in the United States. His efforts did not begin to bear fruit until the resurrection of Albemarle Academy in 1814, and the progression from concept to reality involved struggles with the State Legislature, with site irregularities, and with budget limitations. The resulting architectural masterpiece bestowed a legacy that still survives, the embodiment of the concepts of one man's quest for eternal freedom of the mind and soul, and his models of taste and good architecture are more than ever "furnishing to the student examples of the precepts he will be taught in that art."[95]

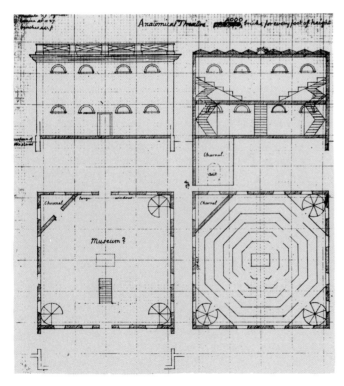

44. Thomas Jefferson. Study for Anatomical Theatre, c. February 1825. Pricking, scoring, iron-gall ink, pencil on laid paper engraved with coordinate lines, 12¼ x 11¼. N-365. Jefferson Papers.

46. William Goodacre, draughtsman, and Fenner Sears & Co, engraver and printer. *University of Virginia, Charlottesville*, 1831. Steel engraving, 3¾ x 5⅝. Published by H.L. Hinton & Simpkin and Marshall. Special Collections, Edwin M. Betts Collection.

JEFFERSON'S LAWN:
Perceptions, Interpretations, Meanings

RICHARD GUY WILSON
Commonwealth Professor of Architectural History, University of Virginia

The University of Virginia is widely hailed as a masterpiece.[1] From around the world visitors arrive to experience the "Lawn," or the "Grounds," which are the local colloquialisms for "Mr. Jefferson's" institution. Frequently cited as one of the most admired examples of American architecture, the University is one of the few American creations that unquestionably ranks with the grand monuments of European history. The attention lavished on the Lawn, which has been a paradigm for the design of other large complexes, can be excessive. And yet to any person who has ventured down the arcades of the ranges, or along the curving garden walls, or around the Rotunda, or who has preferably entered from the south—as Jefferson intended—and viewed the colonnades and pavilions as they sweep in a grand triumphal march up to the Rotunda, all the attention seems warranted. Pictures, photographs, and beautifully worded descriptions can not convey the power, the drama, and yet the calmness imparted by the Lawn. It is not uncommon for viewers to feel a tug of melancholy or awe. Ultimately, however, the experience of the Lawn varies: it speaks on different levels and in different ways to all who use or visit it.

The University of Virginia can be viewed as a summation of Thomas Jefferson's manifold architectural endeavors along with his political concerns regarding the independence of the human mind. Jefferson believed that freedom could only be preserved by an enlightened populace; in 1805, while initially planning a university, he wrote: "I have looked on our present state of liberty as a short-lived possession unless the mass of the people could be informed to a certain degree."[2]

Jefferson and his creations—both intellectual and architectural—have assumed such resonance in the American mind that any consideration of the design and the architecture of the University inevitably involves him both as an individual and as a legend. The University of Virginia consummated his educational concerns. Jefferson's request to place on his grave marker only three of his many accomplishments—"Author of the Declaration of American Independence/of the Statute of Virginia for Religious Freedom/and father of the University of Virginia"—reveals his pride in the University: it culminated his lifelong quest for political and intellectual freedom. And yet, one should remember that Jefferson's educational intent—similar to most institutions of the period—included only a select portion of the population and excluded women and African-Americans. Only the most talented and privileged of young men would proceed to the University. His was not the wider freedom of opportunity for all that we have come to expect in the twentieth century.

The University of Virginia as both an institution and a significant example of architecture has endured, but it has also changed markedly since 1825. As with many great masterpieces, the Lawn is open to various interpretations, eliciting over the years reactions ranging from admiration to dismissal; some hail it uncritically while others question the design and whether it serves its purpose. These perceptions come from many perspectives: visitors, architects who have tried to make additions to the original composition, and historians and critics who have attempted to discover its meanings. The Lawn has been subjected to intense—and continuing—scrutiny; the number of publications that discuss it can overwhelm even the most compulsive bibliophile. The intent of this essay, therefore, is to examine some, not all, of the perceptions and interpretations of Jefferson's Academical Village, as well as some of the alterations and additions to it, and to suggest possible meanings that this multivalent design embodies.

EARLY PERCEPTIONS

Considerations and evaluations of the University's design in the nineteenth century might be graphed as a reverse bell curve: an initial flurry of interest, followed by spotty commentary from 1840 through 1870, and then rising interest toward the end of the century. Interest in the endeavor appeared even before completion of construction when George Ticknor, a professor at Harvard and a member of the Boston intelligentsia, visited Monticello during December 1824. Construction was well advanced, and he described it as "more beautiful than anything architectural in New England, and more appropriate to an university than can be found, perhaps in the world."[3] Ticknor's response is both the earliest by an outsider and the most positive.

Some of Ticknor's evaluation reflects the impact of Jefferson, who was anything but retiring in estimating his creation. Claiming status with the architectural gods, Jefferson, the inveterate correspondent, boasted to Maria Cosway, his aging lady friend in France: "it would be thought a handsome and classical thing in Italy"; and to his friend William Short: "It will be a splendid establishment, would be thought so in Europe, and for the chastity of its architecture and classical taste leaves everything in America far behind it."[4] In many letters Jefferson proclaimed the virtues of the educational institution and the architecture he had created; to Judge Augustus B. Woodward, he expressed hope that the University would influence the "virtue, freedom, fame and happiness" of the prospective students; and he claimed: "The form and distributions of its structures are original and unique, the architecture chaste and classical…."[5] Jefferson died in 1826 believing he had created a leading educational institution and an architectural landmark; now posterity would assess it.

The next architectural evaluation raised problems. The Duke of Saxe-Weimar-Eisenach, Karl Bernhard, published an account of his travels through North America in 1825–26. He found the buildings at the University to be "all new, and yet some of them threaten to fall in," and he criticized the ten pavilions as being irregular and in a "different manner," which prevented the ensemble from having a "beautiful and majestic appearance." He admired the "crooked lines" of the garden walls: "singular but handsome."[6] The next written assessment was no more favorable even though the source is surprising given that his father, the architect Benjamin Henry Latrobe, provided crucial suggestions to Jefferson for the design. John H.B. Latrobe visited Charlottesville in August 1832 and reported: "Mr. Jefferson was certainly not a man of taste and [the University of Virginia] which was built under his direction proves it." Latrobe disparaged the proportions of the architectural orders and thought Jefferson's choices of models were outdated; he also felt the ensemble had "a shabby genteel look, and is already showing marks left by time on its frail materials."[7] A more positive view came two years later when Harriet Martineau, the English writer, visited the area as part of her tour of the West. She discovered to her surprise that the students and faculty were "particularly winning," cordial, and filled with "mutual good understanding which is seldom found in the small society of a college, village-like in its seclusion." The buildings were "singular," and "advantageously crown an eminence," and she admired the "piazza surrounding an oblong square." She also noted that a Gothic chapel was about to be erected at the foot of the Lawn.[8]

Paralleling these early written descriptions, the University began to enter the visual imagination through a series of prints.[9] The earliest were the Maverick engravings—named for the New York engraver Peter Maverick—which represented the ground plan of the University (fig. 41).[10] As Rector Jefferson had commissioned a number of representations in 1821 and had John Neilson draw up a plan, which served as the basis for Maverick's engravings. Several different states of this schematic ground plan appeared over the years, as did numerous variations of a perspective view drawn in 1824 by William Goodacre and published in 1831 by John Hinton in London. The Hinton view depicted the Lawn without the terraces and inserted a colon-

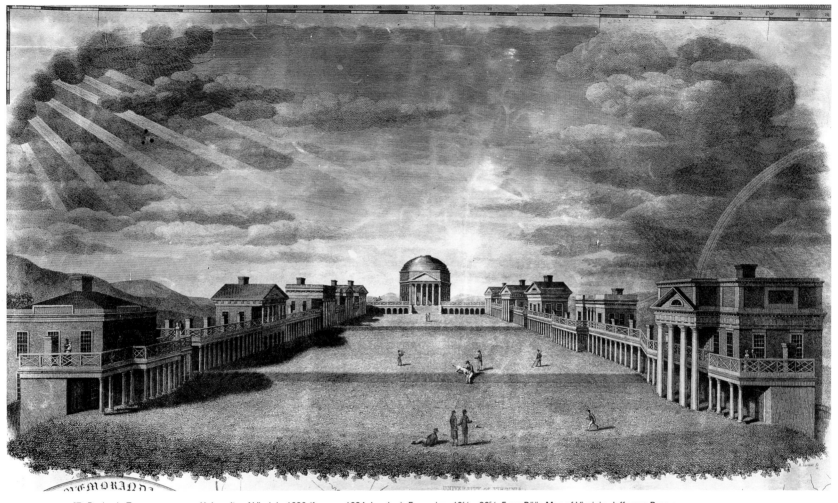

47. Benjamin Tanner, engraver. *University of Virginia*, 1826 (from an 1824 drawing). Engraving, 13⅙ x 26⅝. From Böÿe Map of Virginia. Jefferson Papers.

nade connecting the Rotunda to the wings (fig. 46). Construction was still underway, and apparently Goodacre followed a connecting scheme shown on the Maverick plan that was not built. Similarly, another view of 1824 more accurately showed the terracing and included an arcade across the north end (fig. 47). How many of these different views were published and how widely they were circulated is unclear. In the 1850s came several more views, among them the most famous, an aerial perspective published by Casimir Bohn of Washington, D.C., after the drawing and engraving by Edward Sachse (fig. 48). Drawn from the top of Lewis Mountain, located to the west of the Grounds, it presented a perspective experienced by few visitors. Sachse showed the Lawn planted with trees and the Rotunda with a long wing to the north. Even more impressive (and containing a vast amount of artistic license) was the enlargement of the Rotunda, which looms up more than doubled in size and dwarfs the pavilions, colonnades, ranges, and hotels. The Rotunda dominates the landscape and becomes a topographic feature competing with the nearby mountains. Widely published and reissued over the years—even today it is readily available—the Bohn print became one of the iconic views of the University.

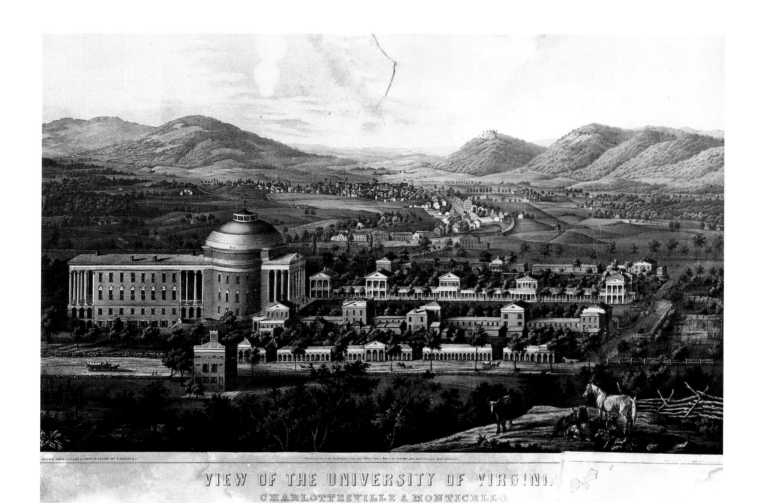

48. Edward Sachse, draughtsman. *View of the University of Virginia, Charlottesville and Monticello, Taken From Lewis Mountain*, 1856. Lithograph, 17¾ X 26⅜. Published by Casimir Bohn, Washington, D.C. Special Collections, Edwin M. Betts Collection.

The long wing, or tail, of the Rotunda was added in 1851–53 by Robert Mills, who had worked with Jefferson in the early 1800s (fig. 49). Known as the Annex, or New Hall, it contained classrooms and a large public hall capable of seating 1,200. New requirements such as large meeting halls not foreseen by Jefferson were changing the University's fabric. Using red brick with white trim, Mills attempted to harmonize with Jefferson's design: he replicated the Rotunda's portico on the north end of his annex, though he substituted cast iron for the capitals of the Corinthian order rather than using marble, as in the original. In spite of its awkward and ungainly appearance,

the Annex was apparently admired by the University community; however, it indicated a problem that continued to bedevil architects: how to make additions to Mr. Jefferson's design.[11]

A few other views of the University, along with commentary, were published in the 1850s, such as those of Porte Crayon, an artist, who took a tour through the Commonwealth for *Harper's*: "The whole [of the University] has a very pleasing and pretty effect, but the buildings are too low and the architecture wants finish."[12] From the late 1850s to the 1880s, the nadir of recognition for the Lawn was reached. This lack of interest is to some degree understandable; travel was difficult, and Charlottesville was relatively inaccessible and not on the main routes. In addition, the center of American publishing was located in the North, the South was frequently viewed as intellectually vacuous, and the University was considered a bastion of the Old South and slavery. And then there was the Civil War. The dark shadow of the war fell across Jefferson's reputation "like a great and furious Nemesis," as Merrill Peterson explains in his study of the Jefferson image.[13] Finally there was the religious issue.

The religious question may be difficult to understand today, but for many individuals in the nineteenth century Jefferson was an "infidel propagandist." His deism and concern with religious freedom caused one agitated Episcopal cleric to claim that Jefferson had erected "an alliance between the civil authority and infidelity," and that the University taught "a refined and civilized heathenism."[14] In actuality, Jefferson explicitly allowed for religious services in the Rotunda, and he proposed that various sects establish divinity schools in proximity to the University. While he created no professorship of divinity, he provided for a chair in Moral Philosophy that would expose students to the great teachings, including those of Jesus. But the University of Virginia stood outside the overwhelming mold of most American institutions of higher learning in the nineteenth century in that it was not religiously based, no chapel dominated the campus, and the University's professors were not men of the cloth. This last issue had been particularly important to Jefferson, and he had sought his faculty among European men of learning, none of whom was a cleric. A Presbyterian minister and a former University student described the Lawn's inhabitants—including professors—as "a most godless set."[15]

The University became a battleground as outsiders, professors, and students sought to bring Christianity onto the Grounds. In 1829 Episcopal Bishop William Meade of Virginia predicted the University's "destruction" when he preached that the "Almighty is angry" at the Rotunda.[16] The result was the appointment in the same year of the University's first chaplain, who

would be paid by voluntary contributions of students and faculty, a system that continued until 1897. The first attempt to add a University chapel came in 1835 when plans were "procured from an architect of high reputation … [for] a church or chapel in the Gothic style" to be placed on the Lawn "immediately in front of the Rotunda."[17] The identity of the architect has vanished along with the plans, however General John Hartwell Cocke gave his blessings to the scheme, calling it "beautiful and appropriate."[18] That Cocke, a member of the original Board of Visitors, a close associate of Jefferson, and the patron of a Jefferson-styled villa at Bremo, agreed to a Gothic-styled chapel on the Lawn indicates the change in religious sentiment in the ten years since Jefferson's death. The chapel campaign struggled on for several years, but funds were never secured. However, the issue persisted, and around 1837

49. Annex or New Hall, 1852; Robert Mills, architect. Plate 46 from Joseph Everett Chandler, *Colonial Architecture of Maryland, Pennsylvania, and Virginia* (1892). Special Collections, Fiske Kimball Fine Arts Library.

50. Receipt acknowledging a subscription to the "U. V. Chapel Fund," showing the elevation and plan for a proposed chapel. William Pratt, draughtsman, 1859. Special Collections.

one of the gymnasia spaces under the Rotunda terraces was converted into a chapel. William McGuffey, an ordained Presbyterian minister, was appointed to the Professorship of Moral Philosophy in 1845 to mitigate the anti-Christian charges, and in 1858 the Young Men's Christian Association, the first at an American college, opened at the University.[19]

This controversy reveals another subtlety of the Lawn: its openness, or to some a seeming emptiness and lack of termination. Many individuals, including architects and faculty, appear to have felt threatened by it, and they proposed huts for statues of Jefferson, buildings, triumphal arches, and chapels, all intended either to fill up or close off that yawning space. [20]

The chapel issue returned to center stage in the late 1850s when William Abbot Pratt, an engineer, landscapist, and architect, became the University's

first Superintendent of Buildings and Grounds. Pratt designed a Gothic chapel for the south end of the Lawn, again facing the Rotunda (fig. 50). A writer in the student newspaper classified Pratt's scheme as "heterogenous architectural hash," an example of "mongrel Gothic," and asked for a "severely Classic" design.[21] However, fund-raising floundered when the Civil War intervened.

The University finally built a chapel in 1885–90. Agitation for it had continued, many clergy feeling that death was preferable for a young man to entering that heathen university. In the early 1880s the Reverend Otis Glazebook, an Episcopalian, galvanized the University community through a fund-raising drive. Much of the funding came through the Ladies Chapel Aid Society. Though the familiar location facing the Rotunda on the Lawn was considered, other sites were discussed, and finally the Board of Visitors selected an area to the northwest of the Rotunda balancing Brooks Hall (the natural-history building, built in 1875–76) on the northeast. Designed by Charles E. Cassell of Baltimore in what he identified as the "early pointed" style, the Chapel was nominally Gothic in the High Victorian mode with its contorted proportions and rough-textured stonework (fig. 51).[22] The ideological implications were obvious, as the University's Professor of Modern Languages, Maximilian Schele de Vere, pointed out in his address at the dedication: "Behind us rise in cold though classic beauty the outlines of a pagan temple…. Before us … the pointed window, the flying buttress, the pointed steeple, … aspiring to heaven."[23] Now at last students had a place to pray, though the question of their relative heathenism would continue, along with attacks on Jefferson as an infidel.[24] With the Chapel's completion, one source of compromise to Jefferson's original design disappeared. However, the Chapel did not really compete with Jefferson's scheme; it existed in its own sphere of influence. Its location, in relation to the earlier Brooks Hall, indicated that a reorientation of the University was taking place: the two buildings were oriented to University Avenue, or the main east-west road, and not to Jefferson's original entry, which had been at the south end of the Lawn. This new perception of entry to the Grounds would become more apparent in the next several years.

DISCOVERY AND INTERPRETATION: ARCHITECTS AND HISTORIANS

In the 1890s historians and architects began to discover the genius of Thomas Jefferson as an architect and to appreciate the importance of his University. If today Jefferson's status as an architect is not questioned, this was not the case in the nineteenth century. In Charlottesville, his role was acknowledged, but nationally, and in the biographies of him, architecture beyond his work at Monticello played almost no part—nor was it seen as a crucial expression of his political and educational interests. The first history of American art, written by William Dunlap and published in 1834, buried Jefferson under the Robert Mills entry, and although Jefferson was cited as the designer of the University, the impression was left that Mills did the general plan and elevations of Monticello.[25] When Jefferson was identified as the architect of the University, as in an 1872 article by Professor de Vere, he was treated as an amateur.[26] Additionally, interest in early American architecture did not arise until the centennial of 1876, and then much of the focus was on New England.

Herbert Baxter Adams, a historian at Johns Hopkins University, published the first reappraisal of Jefferson and the University in 1888. The primary purpose of Adams's study was educational, and he saw Jefferson as a pioneering proponent of modern higher education. Adams recognized that Jefferson had promoted a system of electives rather than a required course of study, that he had understood the multiplicity of areas of specific knowledge and the importance of technical and scientific study instead of a purely classical curriculum, and finally that he had separated the University from religion. Jefferson became for Adams the creator of the modern centralized university, and through the influence of Adams's book, Jefferson's academic policies would play a major role in the establishment and growth of universities in other states beginning in the 1890s.[27]

Adams published several drawings ascribed to Jefferson (they had been redrawn) and gave him full credit for the design of the University: "the very ground-plan and structure of its buildings, every material estimate and every architectural detail, are the work of Thomas Jefferson."[28] Adams's emphasis

51. University Chapel, 1889; Charles E. Cassell, architect. Special Collections, Prints Collection.

52. Fayerweather Gymnasium, 1893-94; Carpenter & Peebles, architects. Special Collections, Prints Collection.

on Jefferson as the designer indicates that skepticism had existed about Jefferson's architectural contributions. Also of importance as a guide to future studies was Adams's inquiry into the origins of Jefferson's design; he cited the Leoni edition of Palladio as the only source. According to Adams, Jefferson's "varying types of classical architecture were copied from well-known Roman buildings, pictured by Palladio," and he spent as much time on the Rotunda, a one-third sized reduction of the "Roman Pantheon, … as did Michael Angelo … upon the dome of St. Peter's." Adams compared features of the plan, especially the colonnades and the single student rooms, to "some ancient monastery … like monkish cells." And he concluded his architectural considerations with this observation: "How charmingly old Rome, mediaeval Europe, and modern America blend together before the very eyes of young Virginia!"[29]

A few years later, John Kevan Peebles, a University alumnus (class of 1890) and an architect in Norfolk, wrote an article on Jefferson's architecture as part of the commentary for his recent building at the University, Fayerweather Gymnasium, 1893, designed with his partner James R. Carpenter (fig. 52). In his article, which was reprinted in the national architectural press, Peebles decried the lack of notice about Jefferson's architectural contributions and described the desecration of the University's plan by the addition of many recent buildings, especially Brooks Hall and the Chapel. For his design of Fayerweather Hall, Peebles claimed: "While no copy of any

Classic structure, … [it] follows the lines laid down by Jefferson."[30]

The University's architecture moved into the public eye with the burning of the Rotunda on October 27, 1895, and the subsequent rebuilding and additions to the Grounds by McKim, Mead & White. The New York partnership of Charles Follen McKim, William R. Mead, and Stanford White was clearly the leading American architectural office of the turn-of-the-century. They espoused a revivified classicism that resulted in an American Renaissance, and they fully sympathized with Jefferson's architectural goals. McKim had designed a seal for the University in 1890 and then visited the Grounds in 1895. A few days after the fire, Mead counseled the head of the University's medical school against selecting unsympathetic architects: "we should consider it an honor to be associated with the work."[31] Hence, when problems were discovered in designs for rebuilding the Rotunda drafted by a hastily selected architect, McKim, Mead & White were natural candidates for the job.[32] From the University's point of view the fire was seen as an opportunity to expand and improve outdated facilities. A report by the faculty to the Rector and Board of Visitors asked not just for restoration, but "to increase its usefulness by providing facilities more ample and splendid than we have heretofore enjoyed."[33]

White played the leading role, traveling frequently to Charlottesville, sometimes accompanied by McKim. Their admiration for Jefferson's design becomes apparent in letters and documents: "The old University buildings surrounding the Campus are the most monumental, if not the most beautiful piece of Colonial architecture in America."[34] White's trepidation about the project is apparent from a conversation with a friend: "'I've seen *his* plans' and then with great deference: 'They're wonderful and I'm scared to death. I only hope I can do it right'."[35] For the Rotunda, White claimed it would "be restored in exact facsimile," the only exterior change being the replacement of the unsightly Annex (where the fire had begun) with a portico "similar to the one on the front … as this was evidently Jefferson's intention."[36] This new northern shallow portico with a "great flight of steps" actually marked a com-

plete reversal of Jefferson's original plan; now the entrance to the Grounds would be from the north (fig. 53). White inserted sorely needed class and office space under the terraces that he extended around the Rotunda, and he constructed the new dome of fireproof Guastavino tile and lengthened its radius, thus slightly raising its profile. White's belief that he could divine Jefferson's intentions led him to revise the interior plan, for as he explained: "only one deviation from the original plan has been made, but this is one which Jefferson would unquestionably have adopted himself had be been able to do so when the Rotunda was built, and one which he would have himself insisted upon still more, could he have directed the restoration." For utilitarian reasons, White argued, Jefferson had divided the interior into two floors, but he had really desired a single two-story space for the Library;

53. Rotunda, North Front, 1896-98; Stanford White of McKim, Mead & White, architect. Special Collections, Prints Collection.

54. Rotunda, Interior, 1896-98; Stanford White, architect.
Special Collections Department, Holsinger Studio Collection.

hence White was respecting what Jefferson could not accomplish (fig. 54). Although White took responsibility for these changes, the Faculty, in a report dated four days after the fire, had specifically requested a new north entrance and the single volume of space for the Library. McKim, Mead & White's Rotunda alterations provided two new visual experiences, both highly dramatic: entry most normally came alongside the Rotunda, through a colonnade that suddenly brought the observer into an awe-inspiring panorama of white columns and greenery; and the view from the terraces surrounding the Rotunda was sublime in its majesty, picturesque in its variety.

McKim, Mead & White's other major area of attention was the closing in of the south end of the Lawn. The Faculty had requested a "new Academical Building" with "a public hall, designed in the horseshoe or theatrical form."[37] They did not specify a location. White submitted two proposals for the placement of new buildings; one at the side of the Lawn "would be the most practical," while the other at the south end "would seem to be the most natural and architectural finish of the group," though "we should regret blocking the beautiful vista at the end of the present campus."[38] He explained his plans to the Faculty's Building Committee and then the Board of Visitors. The Rector, W.C.N. Randolph (Jefferson's great-grandson), directed White to close the Lawn and build at the south end. The reason lay in the fact that Jefferson's southern entry had never worked very well; the slope of the hill was often impossible to traverse in inclement weather. In addition, the area immediately to the south of the University's land and in full view was filled with unsightly houses that the new buildings would block. Jefferson's original idea that his plan would

"admit extension" through a repetition of dormitories, colonnades, and pavilions was impossible.[39] Not only did the topography prevent expansion, but the University did not even own the property; in addition, the setting for higher education had changed from small classrooms to large lecture rooms and laboratory spaces. In any event, a more natural entry lay on the north side of the Grounds.

White separated his buildings from Jefferson's by locating them behind a court measuring three-hundred feet wide and two-hundred feet deep, and graded to a level twenty feet below the bottom step of the Rotunda (fig. 55). He argued that from the Rotunda these new structures—Cabell, Rouse, and Cocke halls—would "appear as only one story in height, whereas on account of the steep grade they actually count for practical use as two." White rationalized his decision: "The charm of the present Close and the domination of the Rotunda are therefore preserved."[40] The Ragged Mountains rising in the distance beyond Cabell Hall could still be seen from the Rotunda. White attempted to continue the Jefferson pavilion model by placing pedimented

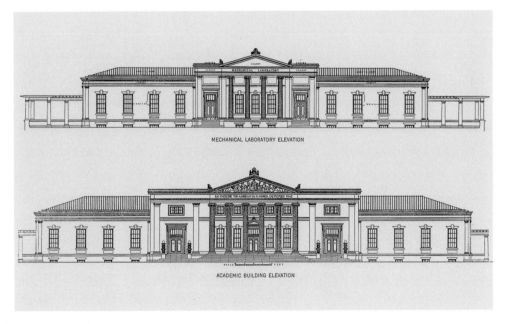

MECHANICAL LABORATORY ELEVATION

ACADEMIC BUILDING ELEVATION

55. Cocke Hall and Cabell Hall, 1896-98; Stanford White, architect. Plate 11 from *A Monograph of the Works of McKim, Mead & White, 1879-1915* (1915-20; reprint, New York: Dover, 1990).

56. Cabell Hall, Auditorium (with copy of Raphael's *School of Athens* by George W. Breck), 1896–98; Stanford White, architect. Special Collections, Prints Collection.

porticos on the new academical buildings. Horizontally massed with lower wings, the familiar red brick and white trim established continuity with the pavilions. Because of the University's economic problems, concrete replaced marble. In the Cabell Hall auditorium, White paid homage to Jefferson by reversing the space; the amphitheater is not placed in the hillside, but rather, the audience enters past the stage and then turns to sit facing the Rotunda (fig. 56). On the wall facing the Rotunda he placed a copy of Raphael's *School of Athens* (a copy had hung in Mills's Annex and had been destroyed in the fire). Cabell Hall's volume is one half of the Rotunda's sphere. White may have blocked the full vista, but he maintained the open central space and the axis running from the Rotunda, recognizing this as the central element of the University plan.[41]

McKim, Mead & White's association with the University continued until 1912. They designed the Power House, 1896–98, Carr's Hill (the president's house), 1906–09, and Garrett Hall, or the Refectory and Commons, 1907–

08. Equally important, the firm prepared a plan for future expansion of the University that envisioned a Beaux-Arts grouping of buildings into courts at the south end on a cross axis (fig. 57). To some degree a few structures such as Randall Hall, 1899, and Minor Hall, 1911, followed this scheme, but most later buildings turned their backs on the Lawn and with minor exceptions need not concern us.

McKim, Mead & White's work was accompanied by increased attention from the architectural community to Jefferson's design, and also controversy concerning his role. Montgomery Schuyler, perhaps the most perceptive of the New York architectural critics and a member of the editorial staff of the *New York Times*, assessed Jefferson's influence on American architecture.[42] Schuyler wrote one of the earliest histories of Colonial architecture in which began the practice of including Jefferson with the early period in spite of the fact that most of his work is post-Colonial. According to Schuyler, Jefferson did not design the Virginia Capitol; rather, "M. Clarissault [*sic*, Schuyler is following Jefferson]" did, but "unquestionably" Jefferson designed the University. He argued that "Considering the resources available for carrying it into execution" and its remote location, "Jefferson's scheme was incomparably the most ambitious and monumental architectural project that had or has yet been conceived in this century." Schuyler criticized elements such as the second-floor porches on the temple-fronted pavilions and his use of wood, and he concluded by noting that Jefferson's taint of "Unitarianism" brought the University into "popular disfavor" for years.[43] In later articles Schuyler returned to the University, heaping even more praise on it and admiring the McKim, Mead & White additions, which he claimed would have met with Jefferson's "approbation": "The style and scale of Jefferson's work are preserved; the material is bettered." The standard explanation of economy for the serpentine brick walls—or as Schuyler explained it, the "translation of the '"Virginia rail fence' into terms of brickwork"—he found questionable. They were too picturesque, too much of a folly, and not appropriate for the formal grandeur of the complex. But he also added, for him, a new note: Jefferson

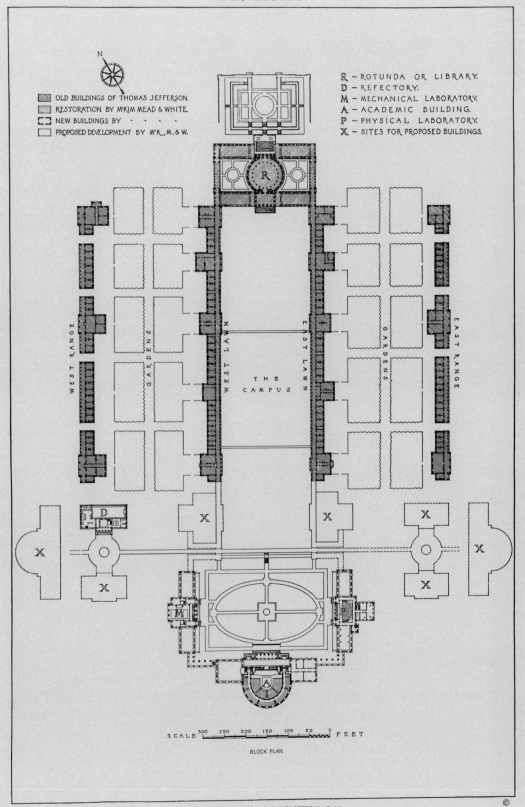

N

OLD BUILDINGS OF THOMAS JEFFERSON.
RESTORATION BY McKIM MEAD & WHITE.
NEW BUILDINGS BY " " " "
PROPOSED DEVELOPMENT BY McK., M. & W.

R — ROTUNDA OR LIBRARY.
D — REFECTORY.
M — MECHANICAL LABORATORY.
A — ACADEMIC BUILDING.
P — PHYSICAL LABORATORY.
X — SITES FOR PROPOSED BUILDINGS.

WEST RANGE

GARDENS

WEST LAWN

THE CAMPUS

EAST LAWN

GARDENS

EAST RANGE

SCALE 300 250 200 150 100 50 0 FEET

BLOCK PLAN

UNIVERSITY OF VIRGINIA, CHARLOTTESVILLE, VA.
1898

57. Plan for the University, ca. 1898-1910; McKim, Mead & White, architects. Plate 110 from *A Monograph of the Works of McKim, Mead & White, 1879-1915* (1915-20; reprint, New York: Dover, 1990).

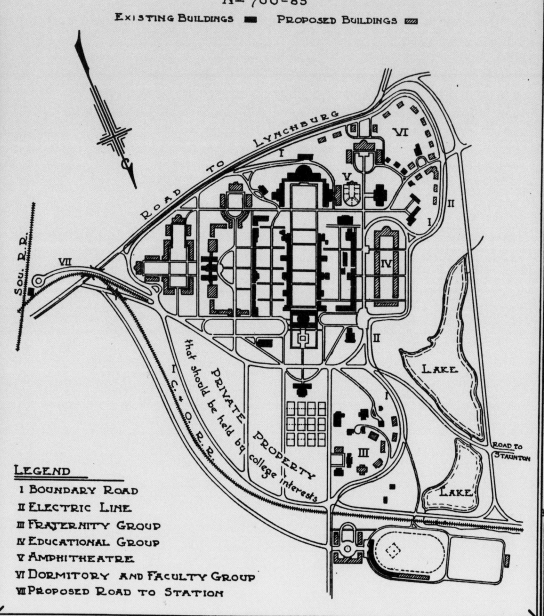

58. Plan for the University, 1913; Warren H. Manning, designer. Plate XXIII from William A. Lambeth and Warren H. Manning, *Thomas Jefferson as an Architect and Designer of Landscape*, (Boston: Houghton Mifflin, 1913). Special Collections, Rare Books Division.

had been assisted by Robert Mills.[44] Schuyler's identification of Mills as having been involved with the University caused confusion that lasted for years.

This concern over who designed what reflected new research on early American architecture, which had received little prior attention, and it also signaled uneasiness that an "amateur," or non-professional, architect could have designed such a complex. The most persuasive evidence came from Glenn Brown, an otherwise knowledgeable architect responsible for considerable research on early Virginia and Washington, D.C., architecture. Initially Brown claimed that letters in the possession of Robert Mills's family indicated "at least a cooperation with Jefferson," but then, in the course of research on the United States Capitol, he discovered Jefferson's correspondence with William Thornton. In a 1913 article, Brown claimed that Thornton had designed the University, not Jefferson.[45]

Although skepticism about Jefferson's role continued for years, for most people the question of primary responsibility and Jefferson's architectural competence came to an end with two books published in 1913 and 1916.[46] The first, by William A. Lambeth, the University's Director of Athletics, and Warren H. Manning, a landscape architect from Boston, was the lesser volume, more of a general defense of Jefferson as an architect. Manning, who had taken charge of the University plan in 1913, provided a superficial overview and included his schemes for expansion with mini-Lawns to the east and west (fig. 58). Lambeth considered the various documents, including the Thornton correspondence, and concluded: "The plan of the University did not full panoplied, leap forth from the brain of Jefferson, but was an evolution out of the meditations of an intellect…."[47]

Far more important was the 1916 folio-sized volume by Fiske Kimball, *Thomas Jefferson, Architect*.[48] Kimball had been trained as an architect under the Beaux-Arts system at Harvard and hence had an appreciation for ordered and classically based designs. Kimball would head the University's first department of architecture—1919 to 1923—and in that role he designed several structures for the Grounds. He later became Director of the Philadelphia

Museum of Art. Always an active scholar, Kimball published voluminously on Jefferson, early American architecture, and other topics.[49] In his heavily illustrated volume on Jefferson, he considered all the known drawings, both at the Massachusetts Historical Society and at the University, and firmly established Jefferson's importance as a designer, although with a qualification: "Though not a professional, he was nevertheless an architect in the true modern sense." The University design was not above criticism, and Kimball noted problems with Jefferson's initial three-equal-sided scheme, his massing and lack of plasticity, and some of the "meretricious ornament," but he lauded his "scientific impulse" and his use of Palladio as representative of an ordered and codified universe.[50]

Kimball's contributions to our appreciation of Jefferson as an architect remain unsurpassed in spite of a voluminous outpouring of books and articles. He delineated a line of scholarly interest that has guided future evaluations of the University and its meaning. Kimball saw Jefferson as an amateur who drew upon various sources: books on architecture from his enormous library, experiences from his travels, and correspondence with Mills, Latrobe, and Thornton.[51] Identifying these sources became one of the major activities of later historians and interpreters.

On a broader level, a battle has been fought over whether Jefferson was more influenced by English or French architecture, and how much of a role his beloved Palladio played. Was Jefferson too much an Englishman, really an Anglo-Palladian in disguise? Or did the revolutionary French architecture he must have observed while in Paris influence him? Kimball spurred the battle by claiming that Jefferson had prefigured the entire international Neo-Classic revival of the late eighteenth and early nineteenth centuries.[52] Jefferson's library was filled with both English and French architectural books. The editions of Palladio that he depended on for the Lawn were primarily English, the Leoni editions; hence he was really working within the British architectural circuit. But alternatively, he also depended on a French book by Fréart de Chambray and Errard for other pavilions on the Lawn.

59. Pavilion IX. (Photograph by Bill Sublette.)

Although the argument can appear banal—and at times has descended into trivial hairsplitting—it can have important consequences, since it involves the question of Jefferson's ideological intentions.

One example can be seen in the facade of Pavilion IX, which has become the most famous and reproduced of all the Lawn facades (fig. 59). This facade is unusual because it lacks a giant order and contains an exedra screened by two Ionic columns *in antis* drawn from Fréart de Chambray. Actually, Jefferson had originally specified the Tuscan order for the niche and entablature but then changed to the Ionic of Fortuna Virilis. On his drawing for the pavilion Jefferson inscribed in two places: "Latrobe." This has been interpreted by some scholars to indicate that Latrobe designed it, and indeed Latrobe did use a similar niche in some of his buildings.[53] Other scholars have traced the niche back to a Parisian house designed by the French "revolutionary," or "visionary," architect Claude-Nicolas Ledoux that was illustrated in a book Jefferson owned (fig. 60).[54] But a recessed niche was not exclusively a

French revolutionary form; many Anglo-Palladians had used it, and Jefferson had also seen it employed in a temple at Stowe. Also, the origins of the exedra stretch back at least to the Roman baths.[55] The conclusion that might be drawn from such an array of sources is that Latrobe probably suggested the recessed motif and that Jefferson, recognizing it as another desirable "specimen" of architecture, adopted it.

Even more of a conflict has erupted over the sources for the ground plan of the University. Kimball initially suggested a broad range of possible influences such as cloisters, forums, and palaestras of the ancients as shown in Palladio via Leoni.[56] None of these was identified as the specific source; rather, he saw them as part of a generalized background. However, a few years later in an article disproving one possibility—a French *Grands Prix* design of 1805 that Jefferson never saw—Kimball introduced the possibility of the chateau and gardens at Marly-le-Roi, which Jefferson had visited in 1786 while in Paris (fig. 61).[57] Composed of a central building at the head of a rectangular garden bordered by six pavilions on each side and connected by

60. Maison de Mademoiselle Guimard Pavilion, 1770; Claude-Nicolas Ledoux, architect. Plate 49 from J. Ch. Krafft and Pierre Nicholas Ransonnette, *Plans, coupes, élevations des plus belles maisons et des hôtels construits à Paris et dans les environs* (Paris, [1801-03]). Special Collections, Rare Books Division.

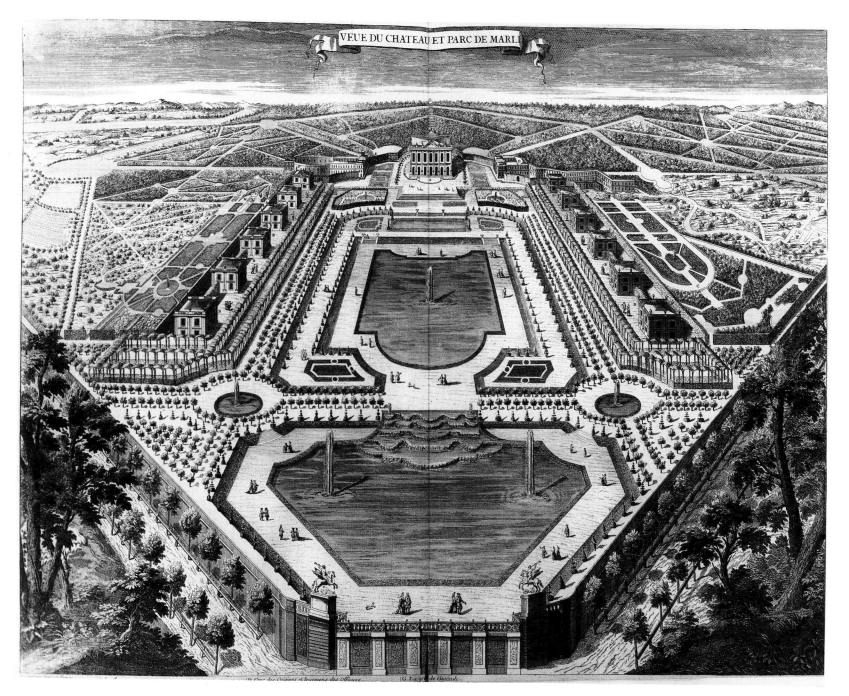

VEUE DU CHATEAU ET PARC DE MARLI

61. Chateau and Gardens of Marly-le-Roi, France, 1679; Jules Hardouin Mansart, architect. Engraving from Gilles de Mortains, *Les Plans, profils, et élevations, des villes, et château de Versailles* (Paris, [1716]). Special Collections, Rare Books Division.

trellises, Marly has been one of the most frequently invoked sources for later historians—in spite of the fact that it was a French royal residence and therefore would hardly have appealed to the staunchly republican Jefferson.[58] To this source have been added: the ground plan of the Hôtel de Salm (now the home of the Legion of Honor) in Paris about which Jefferson wrote movingly; and then, because of Jefferson's concern with health, various French and English plans for hospitals and prisons, as well as college plans in England and the United States.[59] Still other historians have turned back to Jefferson's American origins, noting prototypes such as the village green, Williamsburg, and the domesticated middle landscape of colonial times.[60] All of this speculation on sources reveals the richness of Jefferson's creation, its originality, and how it speaks on different levels.

Fiske Kimball had brought Jefferson and his University design into the American architectural mainstream and had helped initiate a process of canonization. Historians and architects no longer ignored his contributions as an architect, and they increasingly recognized his scheme for the University as a masterpiece. Although to many critics he never quite achieved the innovative stature of Frank Lloyd Wright and Louis Sullivan, still, Jefferson belonged in the pantheon of greats: the first great American architect. To historian Vincent

62. Anatomical Theatre. Special Collections, Edward M. Betts Collection.

Scully, Jefferson's embracing of land, view, and prospect pointed toward the genius of Wright.[61] Even Wright, who seldom had anything good to say about other architects, living or dead, and who dismissed Michelangelo as a "disaster," said shortly before his death: "If Thomas Jefferson were with us, he would be sitting where I am now, at the head of the table."[62] Some historians, though, did take issue: Lewis Mumford felt that Jefferson "went wrong ... and lost sight of his own fundamental principles" with the Rotunda, which he claimed was totally out of keeping with the village plan and should have been integrated with the pavilions instead of showing a deference to "high architectural authority." But "in every other respect," Mumford wrote, "the design is a masterpiece," an "embodiment of three great architectural essentials": a conception of the program for the modern university, unity in the whole, and vitality in details rather than mechanical copying.[63]

Back at the Academical Village, reverence for Jefferson's design remained strong, but as the functional center of the University it became increasingly marginalized. Jefferson's Anatomical Theatre came down in 1939 (fig. 62); it had sat in front of the new Alderman Library building. White's library in the Rotunda had become outmoded and the books were removed. Funds from the Public Works Administration helped revise the Rotunda again in 1938–39; the concrete balustrades and steps of White's "restoration" were replaced with marble.[64] The Lawn continued as the heart of the University, but the Rotunda no longer served much of a purpose except for offices. New construction took place away from the Lawn. In the post-World War II years two University professors of architecture and history, William B. O'Neal and Frederick Doveton Nichols, inherited the mantle of Kimball, and together and individually they brought to light new materials and perspectives on the Lawn.[65] In 1948 the Garden Club of Virginia began funding the restoration of the serpentine walls and pavilion gardens, and then moved on to the area north of the Rotunda, creating a new grand entrance. In the early 1950s Nichols took over direction of the garden work and also began some tentative restoration of the pavilions.

Accompanying the University's canonization was an increasingly harsh scrutiny of additions to the Grounds, especially the alterations of McKim, Mead & White. Their work, at completion and for many years afterwards, had received praise both within the University and from others such as Kimball.[66] But beginning in the 1950s the climate of opinion changed both in Charlottesville and nationally. Henry-Russell Hitchcock, the "dean" of American architectural history, argued that the additions at the end of the Lawn displayed a "lack of understanding," and that in spite of being "'traditional' architects—men who professed the greatest admiration for ... Jefferson ... [they] proceeded to destroy its essence ..." by blocking the great view to the south, thus compromising Jefferson's original scheme.[67]

The result was not the demolishing of the offending buildings—Cabell Hall's auditorium, seating 1,500, was the largest on the central Grounds—but another "restoration" of the Rotunda. In 1955 Nichols began a campaign for returning the Rotunda to Jefferson's design. He

63. Dome Room of Rotunda. Special Collections, Manuscript Division.

convinced the President and the Board of Visitors, and with funds from the Cary D. Langhorn Trust and the Department of Housing and Urban Development the Stanford White interior was removed and a replica of Jefferson's interior was installed in 1973–76. Lack of documentation of the original interior in the form of working drawings and detailed photographs of trim and molding, finishes, and furnishings meant imaginative reinterpretations of many features.[68] White's exterior—the terraces, new portico, and other features—remained, but on the interior one could now grasp the original configuration of the spaces intended by Jefferson for the Rotunda (fig. 63).

Over the years the Lawn had become a hallowed and sacred precinct. Students still lived in the dormitory rooms, but Jefferson's concept that the ground floors of the pavilions would be classrooms had never been successful, and they had been converted into faculty residences, a club, and offices. An earnest restoration program began in the 1980s under the direction of an architect for the historical buildings, James Murray Howard. Pavilion VIII, which had served as the President's office for years, was restored on the ground floors for teaching; and so once again classes—in a minimal way—returned to the Lawn.

The increased reverence for the Lawn by the broader architectural community, although certainly genuine, sprang from an intense anti-modernist strain that began in the 1960s and that called for a return to traditional architectural forms. A new concern with the city and its deterioration, and also with suburban sprawl, led many architects and historians to invoke the Lawn as a paradigm for the city, despite the irrelevancy of the comparison.[69] The culmination of the Lawn's canonization came during the Bicentennial when the American Institute of Architects ranked the University as the most admired achievement of American architecture.[70] And this has been followed with even more accolades.

With canonization came changes in the interpretation of the Lawn, which was adopted by architects not only for new universities, colleges, and study centers, but also for businesses. Even more striking, the association of the University's architecture with paganism disappeared, and it became a model for religious structures. The Reverend Jerry Falwell announced in 1987 that his proposed new church in Lynchburg would be modeled on Jefferson's Rotunda, "only larger."[71]

MEANINGS

The history of the Lawn in the 168 years since its completion indicates the changing perceptions of the past and the manifold meanings that can be imbedded in great works of architecture. The various speculations and interpretations concerning the Lawn testify to its importance. But certain points provide meanings for today and thus deserve more emphasis.

Thomas Jefferson was intensely interested in theories and ideals, but he avoided cosmic philosophizing and never attempted to reduce his thought to one specific system. He was an eclectic who drew constantly from many sources in political theory, education, and architecture.[72] He sought unities and found some that today we might not accept, but he recognized that knowledge constantly evolved.[73] Jefferson did not espouse rigid doctrines and static systems; instead, he retained an openness to new ideas, a belief in progress and in the future.[74] Although he praised the ideal, he always maintained a view of the practical. Jefferson enjoyed the arts and the art of living well, but a utilitarian streak underlay everything: pure frivolity and silly speculation never entered his philosophical thinking. He dismissed Plato as filled with "whimsies" and "nonsense," and although he recommended several ancient moralists, among them "Jesus of Nazareth" as the most sublime and benevolent, there is a presentness to Jefferson's thought, a search for what would work today and tomorrow.[75] Jefferson read history, frequently com-

64. Bodleian plate showing the College of William and Mary, ca. 1732-47, detail. (Named for the Bodleian Library, Oxford University, where it was discovered.) Colonial Williamsburg Foundation.

menting upon it, and believed it offered lessons, but it was ridiculous to tie actions to ancestors and past behaviors: knowledge had improved.[76] "Science is progressive," he observed, "what was useful two centuries ago is now become useless."[77] Jefferson respected the past, whether political or architectural, for what it could teach but not for how it could be duplicated. He admired Palladio, especially the Leoni edition, but he was as averse to using this as his only architectural source as he was reluctant to use any single literary source for his politics.[78]

Dumas Malone sums up his magisterial biography with the observation that Jefferson was "rooted in his native soil."[79] Indeed, formative to Jefferson's ideas for the University were his own youthful experiences, especially at the College of William and Mary. During the years of his attendance, 1760–62, the College was housed in a large building more than sixty years old that is sometimes attributed to Sir Christopher Wren.[80] In this single structure all of the students lived, ate, and attended classes.[81] In front of it stood two houses: the President's and the Bafferton, where a handful of Americans Indians stayed (fig. 64). During Jefferson's tenure, constant uproar characterized the College, which was controlled by the Anglican church. Six of the seven faculty members (as well as the President) were clergymen, and all were embroiled in battles with the local political authorities over their pay, which came from taxes. As upstanding examples to the community, the clergymen failed: supposedly celibate, they fathered illegitimate children, several were drunkards, and one even led the college boys in a raid against the town. The William and Mary students as a whole were out of control, dissipated, and frequently involved in brawls.

Later biographers have speculated that some of Jefferson's animosity towards state-sponsored religion and its involvement in education might have begun during his youth in Albemarle County, but William and Mary certainly determined it.[82] Although Jefferson fondly remembered his one non-clerical professor, William Small, and his later studies with George Wythe, he never expressed any admiration for the College. During his term as Governor he severed the College's ties to the Church. Its architecture he despised as "indifferent accommodation," "rude, mis-shapen."[83] Many academic and architectural features of the University of Virginia, as well its siting, were Jefferson's reaction to his collegiate experience in Williamsburg.

At the University of Virginia, however, Jefferson found his hopes initially thwarted. As an institution the University got off to a rocky start when it opened in 1825. Several of the original professors who were courted and imported from Europe disliked their accommodations in the pavilions and loathed the poorly prepared students; they soon left. The students were not just ignorant, some were drunken louts who created near riots on the Lawn, destroying property and inflicting injury. This reminded Jefferson of Williamsburg, and when as Rector he faced the students in the Rotunda, "his feelings overcame him, and he sat down," unable to speak.[84] Unfortunately after Jefferson's death in 1826 the problem of student behavior continued to plague the University (as it did most American universities); the killing of a professor by a student in 1840 helped bring about creation of the famous honor code in 1842.[85]

Education was the reason for the University: it was designed as the capstone of the Commonwealth of Virginia but also as an example for other states. Jefferson intended it to be "the most eminent in the United States, in order to draw to it the youth of every State, but especially of the south and west."[86] His educational scheme had problematic aspects: the number of disciplines represented was arbitrary, growing from six to ten with the passage of the State enabling act.[87] Jefferson tried to dictate in some areas, for example allowing only certain "approved" texts for the study of government.[88] In many specifics the University has changed over the years; for instance, bachelor's degrees are offered instead of merely diplomas, as Jefferson had envisioned. He certainly would be surprised at the proliferation of degrees, the number of disciplines, and the different methods of instruction. Jefferson, who had sought unities, saw the splintering of knowledge through the growth of science and specialized expertise. Symbolically he had revealed this split with the different pavilions, but then reconciled the differences by the device of a village that culminated in the Rotunda.

Jefferson liked control. He sought to order his life and his environment wherever he lived: Philadelphia, Paris, Charlottesville.[89] He admired nature yet tried to control that portion nearest to him. He had an aversion to cities, not just because of economic policy and fear of the mob, but also because architecturally they were impossible to order, and they contributed to health problems. When asked about the design of cities, Jefferson questioned whether "we ought not to contend with the laws of nature, … all our cities shall be thin-built," and he recommended that they should be laid out on a checkerboard plan leaving alternative squares open for trees.[90] Although later in life Jefferson's position on cities changed, at heart he remained an agrarian, more in sympathy with the tiller of the soil upon whom he had lavished praise in much of his writing.[91] Young men should not be placed in "populous cities, because they acquire there habits and partialities which do not contribute to the happiness of their after life."[92] Hence, he placed the University beyond Charlottesville, not even trusting that small town.

Jefferson's prototype lay in the village, a form he grew up with, created, and saw all about him. The term "village" was how he initially explained his concept of the University.[93] In the Virginia mode of living, the plantation was frequently referred to as a "village."[94] In addition, Karl Lehmann has cited the Roman villa as an inspiration for Jefferson's Monticello and ultimately for the University.[95] Although specific visual and functional connections between them can be disputed, the ideological framework is compelling: the mixture of farm and books, of healthy rusticity and intellectual urbanity, of trees and plantings in a controlled architectural setting. Pliny, Horace, and Cicero portrayed compelling descriptions of intellectual life in the country, and Jefferson's notion of an Academical Village comes out of this background: it was an architectural type much more comprehensible and capable of being ordered. The village became a metaphor for an organization of architectural elements and also of knowledge.

Jefferson was also well aware that the common method of designing large groups of buildings was to create a hierarchical ordering consisting of a central structure and symmetrically disposed dependencies. Scholars have identified the various foreign sources—gardens and hospitals—that served as possible origins for the University's plan, as it was a type of ordering he had already used extensively, for instance at Monticello.[96] Of course his original university village scheme (figs. 3, 4) bore little resemblance to European prototypes.

Jefferson, as did many architects, made a design and then discussed it with colleagues—such as Thornton and Latrobe—and incorporated their suggestions. The critical issue for the University lay with practicality: the site could not accommodate his scheme, which called for 700–800 feet between the two wings, so he changed it to fit the circumstances. Therefore, that it resembles Marly-le-Roi is the result of site, not design. Jefferson saw his University plan as an integral arrangement in which architecture provided communication around an essential central space.

Of Jefferson as a classicist much has been said: the "greatest" and the "first" according to Scully.[97] Jefferson recognized a connection between the classical language and his ideals for political virtue in America, and he sought to give dignity to the civic landscape. But he was never an "aesthetic classicist"; he knew the dark side, that virtue and vice could commingle. Although Jefferson followed some of the rules of the ancients, he changed and modified them as necessary. He never attempted to make reconstructions of ancient buildings, as did many of his contemporaries, and as he had read about in his library.[98] Jefferson adapted elements of celebrated ancient structures such as their fronts, but then placed modern functions inside. Observers have long noted the asymmetry of the Lawn. Composed about an axis, the two sides vary, and the pavilions are not identical. Similarly, Jefferson accommodated the site's slope by making the gardens larger on the east than the west. There is overall order and a repetition of elements: the Tuscan colonnade on the Lawn, the arcades on the ranges. But there are differences in the facades

65. Rotunda and Pavilions VII, V, III, and I. (Photograph by Bill Sublette.)

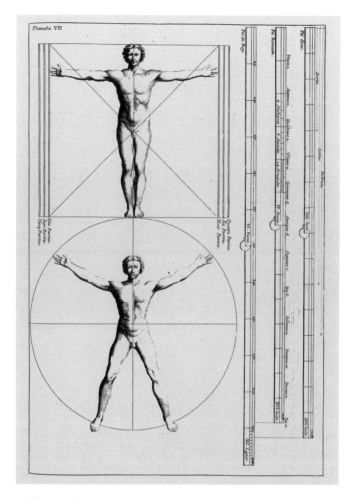

66. Vitruvian Man inscribed in circle. Vitruvius Pollio, *Les dix livres d'architecture de Vitruve corrigez et traduits nouvellement en françois, avec des notes et des figures*, trans. Claude Perrault (Paris, 1684). Special Collections, Rare Books Division.

Jefferson understood the symbols he chose; the best models of antiquity contained meanings. He based the Rotunda, as the Capitol in Richmond, on Roman models that had been assigned by authorities as belonging to the Republic, not the Empire, which he would have found repugnant.[102] Jefferson admired many classical buildings and gardens in Europe, including those of royalty, but his use of them as models always included a change of purpose. Palladio expressed the laws of nature in mathematical terms that appealed to Jefferson. But in execution he realized that not everything could be so reduced; he adapted as necessary, stretched proportions as with the dormitory colonnade, combined and changed in his typically pragmatic fashion. Jefferson belonged to his time: classicism was the language of architecture, but it was elastic and was as capable of change and growth as knowledge.

The new Greek architecture that the younger architects were espousing did not interest Jefferson. An old man when he designed the University, he had an insular quality in his later years and consequently returned to what he knew, the older translations of Palladio and not new editions. To him Roman architecture expressed an authority of time and knowledge that was sufficient to his purpose.

Jefferson capped the Grounds with the Rotunda. Latrobe had suggested it, and Jefferson acknowledged his contribution on the drawings. Since Latrobe's other drawings are lost, the exact development of the design and the relative responsibilities may never be known. But between Latrobe's surviving sketch and Jefferson's drawings many changes can be observed, as Jefferson made it his own. He openly acknowledged its source in the Pantheon. The name came from the Leoni edition of Palladio which referred to "the Pantheon, now call'd the Rotonda," and during construction it was frequently referred to as the "Pantheon."[103] Jefferson considered the Pantheon the most perfect specimen of "spherical" architecture, but he modified it in many ways: windows are inserted, and the portico is only six columns across, as Latrobe had suggested, not eight as in Rome.[104] He reduced the two pediments of the Roman example into one, and the portico is joined to

of the pavilions: "no two alike so as to serve as specimens for the architectural lecturer."[99] Jefferson did not try to associate the different pavilions with the disciplines they might house; their design was a separate process that went through many revisions. Down the Lawn copies of the ancient orders from Fréart de Chambray and Errard are opposed by modern copies from Palladio, but they are not lined up all to one side; instead they are intermixed.[100] And then against the cubical forms of the pavilions sits the "spherical" of the Rotunda.[101]

the cylindrical form by the embrace of a thick entablature. Jefferson (and Latrobe?) treated the portico as an integral compositional element and not as an afterthought (or addition) as in Rome. Instead of a belfry, cupola, or steeple, which commonly appeared on American collegiate buildings and where the clock and/or bell would be placed, Jefferson conceived of something different. For the pediment he ordered a clock from Simon Willard of Boston, and he designed a forked extension so that a bell could be hung above it, a very unorthodox idea. Clocks and bells have a long history as civic symbols, and as organizers of the day they emphasize the order Jefferson struggled to attain. The Rotunda is raised up on a flight of steps, it does not sink, as portrayed in Leoni and as in Rome. A sublime effect is created by the great Corinthian order of the Rotunda and by its height and size, especially when seen in comparison to the pavilions (fig. 65).

The interior of the Rotunda has little to do with the Roman source. Sensuous and plastic curving walls encompass two levels of classrooms, and an awkward stair climbs up one side to the library beneath the dome. The interior—especially today, when it is painted white—is light-filled, clear, and spacious, and in the Dome Room it opens to the sky above. Jefferson knew that the Pantheon was originally a pagan temple of worship, the form of which, according to Leoni, "bears the figure of the World, or is round."[105] Through applied art and decoration, the dome frequently came to represent heaven or the cosmos. And the dome had been appropriated for several of the greatest structures of Christianity. Jefferson, wary of cosmology, transformed the dome into a library, into a temple of enlightenment for education. Significantly, he intended the concave ceiling to function as a planetarium; it would be painted blue and spangled with gilt stars that would be changeable; and Jefferson, always the tinkering inventor, designed a complicated movable seat for the operator.[106] The dome of heaven became an instrument of modern science, and revelation was to be replaced with empiricism in a true spirit of enlightenment.

The importance of the spherical and circular lay not just in ancient pro-totypes such as the Pantheon, but also in their status (along with the cube and square) as the perfect forms: nothing could be added or taken away. The symbolic nature of the circle was further enhanced by the Vitruvian belief that the human form could be inscribed in a circle. Jefferson owned a French edition of Vitruvius that illustrated this concept (fig. 66).[107] In his scheme, the human is at the center, and the library is the mind of the University—the repository of wisdom, knowledge of the past, and ideas for the future.

Still, one must return to the overall scheme and to the space itself that stretches out from the Rotunda to the south, or alternatively, that begins at the bottom of the Lawn and concludes with the Library, and also to the pavilions, dormitories, colonnades, hotels, and ranges, which are part of the overall logic. Jefferson saw the educational system as an assemblage of functions, differentiated but coordinated. Similarly, the white columns of different sizes give a harmonious appearance to the ensemble, although the intervals between the pavilions are irregular. The distance across the Lawn is constant at the top as at the bottom—two hundred feet—but the intervals between the pavilions widen toward the south.[108] The reason for this irregularity lies not with Jefferson having designed in perspective—he did not—but with the constraints of the site and the need to provide more pavilions for the professors. The result, though, combined with the forty-two-inch drop of each terrace, creates a foreshortened appearance, so that the distance to the Rotunda appears greater from the south. Alternatively, from the Rotunda the south end and the last pavilions appear closer. However, there are other accesses to the Lawn as well—up the alleys between the gardens, and here the rigidity of the classical forms of the central portion is offset by the serpentine curves of the brick walls. The gardens provide another mode, quiet and contained, the repose of the ancient Horace. Thus Jefferson created a constantly changing repertory of experiences, of visual and physical stimulus (figs. 67, 68). Contained in the variety of spaces are communication, habitation, study, and learning, both public and private. The spaces are controlled but open, and the orientation is multi-focal: the Rotunda dominates one end, but the central space is not just oriented to the south and the mountains beyond but also to the sky. Jefferson's original plan showed trees in an open square, and happily some trees were planted in the 1830s. Sometimes criticized for blocking views of the pavilions, they are essential; they continue the dialogue Jefferson set up: the manmade and the natural, brought into accord.

The architecture does have a certain tentativeness that some have criticized as insubstantial. Kimball believed that the University showed Jefferson's earlier "colonial manner" from which he never broke.[109] Indeed Jefferson did not look at the latest fashion; his sources were dated. Brick was considered too lowly a material for important monuments or institutions, but he had only brick at his disposal, and that was all the workmen knew how to handle other than wood. But in this common building material a democratic quality emerges; it is capable of assuming noble proportions and intentions, it is honest, and it can be made into columns and other forms. This clearly is a space of the new world, a new American approach, and not a duplicate of the old world or the past.

Thomas Jefferson designed the University of Virginia as a summation of his architectural, scholarly, educational, and political thought. It resembles him as an individual: sometimes contradictory, open to new ideas, looking to the past, and believing in the future. The University is also the product of many years and much thought, not just by Jefferson and his fellow members of the Board of Visitors, but also by Thornton and Latrobe, by John Neilson and James Dinsmore, and by the work of many builders, white and black.

Jefferson saw the design and erection of the complex as crucial to his educational goals: he would not allow it to open half-completed. He believed the architecture to be part of the educational component of the University. For the future leaders of the democratic republic he hoped to attract, the buildings and spaces would be essential; from the architecture would flow an education in taste, values, and ideals. Today the Lawn is the heart of the University, but it is no longer the center of activity. The Rotunda sits not as an integral part of the educational system but as a symbol, a shrine, a museum. Jefferson's idea of an Academical Village has entered the language as a metaphor, not just for architectural parts, but also for separate disciplines, and more recently for the "electronic village" of the computer, fax, modem, and other technologies used by the University community. The question of whether the University has performed the high task Jefferson set for it, and whether the architecture has performed well or is outmoded, will receive any number of answers. Functionally, the Lawn is probably outmoded; but as an ideal and inspiration it still speaks loudly. That it has endured is testimony to its power. The Lawn is an architectural embodiment of, and a challenge to, Jefferson's quest for individual achievement and unlimited freedom.

67. Serpentine Garden Walls. (Photograph by Bill Sublette.)

68. View of West Lawn Colonnade. (Photograph by Bill Sublette.)

69. Rotunda from the South. (Photograph by Bill Sublette.)

THE ACADEMICAL VILLAGE TODAY

JAMES MURRAY HOWARD, AIA
Architect for the Historic Buildings and Grounds, University of Virginia

The foregoing essays have addressed a sequence of events representing almost two hundred years of change and pertaining to the lifespan of the Academical Village. This period began with Jefferson's inspiration for a new type of intellectual community and with the creation of that dream while he still lived. That first blossoming was followed by an era of quiescence, architecturally speaking, and then by several decades of alterations that were often erratic in form and quality. The buildings were simply regarded as real-estate holdings comprising the University of Virginia. Most notably, the Mills addition to the Rotunda in the 1850s radically changed its nature, as did the McKim, Mead & White work on the interior in the 1890s. In 1916, when Fiske Kimball's *Thomas Jefferson, Architect* was published, the first major victory in reestablishing Jefferson's architectural reputation was won. And by the 1970s, when the Rotunda was reconfigured internally to resemble the original arrangement of spaces, the national reverence for Jefferson emerged full-blown, as the Academical Village easily gained acknowledgment as the most outstanding architectural achievement in this country since 1776. After almost two hundred years the image of the place was surprisingly true to that of the early years (figs. 69, 42). Then … a pause.

In the 1980s the University of Virginia faced a dilemma: determining the University's proper role as steward of this superb cultural legacy and the steps that should be taken to arrest the decline of Jefferson's buildings. During this same period Jefferson's international importance to American culture and history was emphatically pronounced with the naming of the Academical Village and Monticello to the World Heritage List.[1] Proper stewardship was no longer merely an option; it was now the only possible course of action. In acknowledging its responsibility to safeguard the site, the University took several steps. It began earnest discussions with the state government of Virginia to explain the need for increased financial support. As a result, some of the worst cases of decrepitude were stabilized to halt increasingly rapid decay. In 1983 the University appointed an Architect for the Historic Buildings and Grounds—a new position—to direct a comprehensive analysis of the condition of the buildings and to begin preservation work. Shortly thereafter the University created the Jeffersonian Restoration Advisory Board, a group of some twenty-five leaders in preservation and philanthropy that would serve as the institutional parent of the movement. Under their aegis, more than ten million dollars in grants, gifts, and government aid have been amassed or pledged to the restoration program, for immediate use or as endowment for long-term support. The philosophical underpinnings of this work have been nurtured by a smaller group of board trustees known as the Design Committee. The Board's two imperatives—funding and a preservation conscience to go with it—have found their rightful places in the University's understanding of its cultural and historical mission.

BELIEFS GUIDING THE RESTORATION PROGRAM

The philosophy guiding stewardship of the Academical Village begins with the belief that Jefferson's ensemble is both a physical artifact of major historical significance and the manifestation of a highly aestheticized yet still vital educational plan. It is essential to keep both attitudes in view at all times, to let neither dominate. This balanced approach is a reaction to a romantic notion of the past wherein dream-like memories of the Lawn setting were revered while the place was allowed to fall into serious physical decay.

The second precept, and one that surprises many, is that the setting is not, and never should be, a museum. It is a living community that has been in continuous use since 1825, when classes were first held. If the buildings, the central terraced greenspace, or the gardens were isolated, it would violate the most compelling of Jefferson's reasons for designing a heterogeneous, tightly knit community of faculty and students. This place inspires and instructs through repeated use in everyday life; it is neither stage set nor museum piece.

By the 1970s preservation professionals in America had generally agreed that stewardship of historic sites, whether museum properties or not, should move away from romanticized attitudes about historic places toward more exact understandings based on thorough research and objective analysis of historic data, current conditions, and preservation options. Such an outlook is in accord with venerable international preservation creeds such as the Venice Charter, which as early as 1931 espoused a more clinical approach than had been customary in the nineteenth century. At its best, application of the Charter and similar dicta allows archaeological evidence to remain intact. Unrestrained exercise of one's will to create and alter can be so destructive to historic sites that their value is severely compromised. Thus, the Design Committee requires of itself a strong measure of ego suppression; the facts of a building and its history must be allowed to speak for themselves. Good stewardship is, in one sense, merely good caretaking.[2]

Finally, the philosophy guiding the present restoration program incorporates educational imperatives directed at several audiences. The most obvious audience is the collection of residents and colleagues who use the place each day. The pavilions still house faculty, and students still live in the small rooms between the pavilions. The Rotunda still serves as a magnet for students, faculty, and an increasing number of visitors. The gardens and grassy terraces continue to enchant the passerby. So where is the educational value

for all these people? It lies in the sophisticating influence of Jefferson's rarefied architectural ensemble, which he had borrowed from antique sources with the precise motive of offering instructional models of architecture at its best. For those who did not grow up amidst the architectural glories of Europe, he built corresponding models close at hand. As long as it stands, the Academical Village will never lose this capacity to teach by affording simple, everyday exposure to utilitarian art. More explicit forms of teaching are also possible, especially in relation to preservation of the setting. To preservation professionals, faculty, and students, the buildings and landscape offer unparalleled opportunities for research in primary and secondary resource materials, and for archaeological examination of conditions that in many instances have survived untouched from Jefferson's day. While documentary study and stylistic analysis common to art history have long found a warm reception within the University, it is only in the past decade that the study of building fabric—which requires working with one's hands at the site—has been offered to students (fig. 70). Again, the desire is to reconnect in whatever way possible with the pedagogical motive upon which Jefferson founded this university. We believe that he would also approve of the fact that his setting has become a laboratory for nurturing preservation students and craftspersons as they prepare for professional lives in a realm of architectural endeavor scarcely envisioned in his lifetime.

As the Design Committee has assessed conditions and opportunities for work each year, it has developed a series of practical guidelines:

1. Assess all historical evidence before making decisions about the property.

2. Fit the present use of the property to the specific historic conditions at hand, rather than radically alter historical conditions to accommodate passing notions. Once altered, archaeological conditions are of little value to future generations. Where alteration uncovers original conditions, action may indeed be very helpful.

70. Pavilion II: student intern Ashley Robbins restoring entablature decoration, July 1991. (Photograph by Martha Tuzson Stockton.)

3. Be as gentle as possible in carrying out intrusive research or alterations that might compromise the historic value of the place.

4. Where intrusion or alterations are necessary to accommodate current users, do so cautiously, respecting both user and artifact. Rarely can a building be all things to all people.

5. Strive to be as inclusive of as many audiences as the historic fabric can allow. For example, certain buildings or areas are more readily accessible to those with disabilities than others; some defy one's best efforts to provide universal access.

6. Let present work be planned in such a way that major interventions will not be necessary with each change of occupants, thereby reducing stress on the fragile and irreplaceable relic. On average, major work should occur every forty years, minor work every ten years.

7. In accordance with research of historic data and programmatic building needs, determine the best way to reveal as much as possible about early conditions that have been changed or hidden from view. The motive should be to give present-day viewers the clearest possible image of Jefferson's architectural intent in terms of building shapes, interior spatial configurations, finishes, and decorative details.

8. To render the buildings usable, some past alterations might be worthwhile, even desirable. Therefore, simple erasure of all past changes is not the aim. Reverse only those changes that are at odds with Jefferson's aim to have architecture that is handsome, well-built, and uplifting. And where awkwardness occurred in Jefferson's own day, keep those examples intact as chapters of the complete story each building must continue to tell.

9. To recreate early conditions, use evidence from this site rather than borrow evidence of the same general period from other sites which could lead to confusion among future researchers.

10. When new features are introduced, make them as passive in design as possible, neither competing for attention with original features nor confusing the viewer about what is old and what is new. The old and new should live harmoniously in both style and quality.

11. As the past is revealed, develop a cadre of skilled craftspersons who can adapt themselves to the techniques appropriate to these buildings. Especially important are techniques common in Jefferson's time but unused or radically different today.

12. Assure that all work is reversible, so that basic artifactual evidence will remain intact for future study.

13. Keep in mind that resuscitation of the Academical Village provides an ideal laboratory setting for those interested in the history of Jefferson and his community, as well as those interested in state-of-the-art techniques of conservation and restoration. The goal should be finesse—in methods of research, in analyzing the resource, and in curing the physical problems.

14. To assist future caretakers of this historic place, thoroughly document all that has been done.

DISCOVERIES AND ACTIONS

Since the early 1980s documentary research and examination of building evidence have yielded much information. Primary written sources have included minutes of Board of Visitors meetings and the Proctor's Papers, as well as letters between Jefferson and his friends and workers. So far, as work has transpired at the pavilions, the drawings for the Academical Village or portions of it have served to elucidate Jefferson's general thought processes and grand ideas, but they have rarely provided exacting detail. This situation is in direct contrast to Monticello, where a much more extensive collection of drawings and corresponding notes remains. The richest findings have been revealed as the buildings of the University have been examined and as conditions long hidden from view have been uncovered.

Among the recent discoveries of most consequence have been details of Jefferson's techniques for installing metal roofing, a growing body of knowledge about early finishes and decorative techniques, evidence of major interior changes, and facts about original hardware and features encapsulated by later work. In the absence of records describing early conditions or subsequent changes, such unanticipated information allows the physical truth to clear up vague notions about what *might* have been and offers a measure of certainty to many decisions that must be made. The single greatest result of research during the 1980s has been the clarification of our image of the ten pavilions, so that we can confidently say that the public is seeing the buildings in a truer, more faithful rendition. Such an approach is more conservative than would have been customary fifty years ago, when restoration was based on generalized understanding of a period or style as distinguished from knowledge of site-specific data.

The first major contact with hidden conditions at the pavilions occurred in 1985 at Pavilion VIII. Early sketches and site study indicated that the entry just outside the front door had been altered. A narrow bridge from the colonnade deck, linking the deck with the second-floor hallway, had been widened, probably in 1854 or 1855, thereby preventing light from spilling downward to the main doorway (fig. 71). Removal of material thought to have been added revealed carved moldings that confirmed the nature of the deck's original design; irregularities in adjacent brickwork answered many other questions. However, the design of the railing panels between deck and handrail remained a mystery. It was decided to rely on Jefferson's repeated use elsewhere of

71. Pavilion VIII: restoration of original bridge between colonnade deck and second floor entry, 1985. (Photograph by Clay Palazzo.)

wooden railings in the manner of Thomas Chippendale's geometric studies, which had been inspired by Oriental motifs. This was the only conjectural feature in an otherwise provable restoration of an altered condition.

While this work was being done, another early condition was exposed: small bands of evidence suggesting that the plaster coating on Jefferson's brick columns had neither been painted nor sand-finished, in contrast to columns at Monticello. The bands remained only because of the widening of the bridge. The column finish that was exposed seemed to contradict the use of brilliant white paint throughout the Academical Village. At that stage in our work, the ramifications of changing the tonality of the entire precinct were considered so profound, both in terms of public reaction and overall cost, that the evidence was left exposed, yet protected, for further analysis and debate as more research is carried out in the future. It is generally felt that the use of brilliant white came about later in the nineteenth century, perhaps during the Greek Revival period.

Pavilion VIII also offered a look at Jefferson's early wood roofing system, which had been used above student rooms and, as later research has shown, on Pavilions V and VIII.[3] The design of these shallow-pitched roofs was incompatible with the conditions of climate and vegetation to which they were subjected, probably causing the roofs to leak even during the first years of occupancy. All the pavilions were soon covered by more serviceable roofs far different in form, and in the process the older leftover roofs underneath were damaged. But much of the original Pavilion VIII roofing was intact, awaiting exploration as researchers entered the upper attic space. After work was completed in 1986, most of that early material still remained in place, protected for future generations of analysts.

A final comment about Pavilion VIII has to do with its function. At the outset all the pavilions served as both classrooms and residences, but over the years students and faculty lost access to them. In 1986, at the suggestion of the University's Committee on Residential Life, classes were reintroduced to Pavilion VIII. Since then it has served as a constant reminder of Jefferson's unique concepts regarding the intermingling of students and faculty, and it has also offered them an inspiring educational experience in the setting Jefferson originally intended.[4]

While restoration of Pavilion VIII was still underway, Pavilion III was ready for similar work, but as a residence without classroom space. On the exterior roof, leakage had caused extensive decay of the wood entablature, necessitating replacement of some members and restoration of elements that could be saved (fig. 72). As one of only two pavilions having no major extensions into its garden, this pavilion had experienced several episodes of interior change during earlier efforts to achieve a more commodious spatial arrangement.

Two of the alterations stand out. The most extensive involved removal of a windowless room on the second floor. The room had been created by the extension of a corridor from the stair at the rear northwest corner of the building to the parlor, at the southwest corner. The corridor's route had flanked the north wall and much of the east wall. Thus a windowless room of moderate size, huddled against an irregularly shaped central chimney mass, had been created. Later the positions of corridor and room were reversed, producing a room with windows and a windowless corridor winding its way awkwardly between rooms. Evidence of the original wall locations appeared as darkened floor varnishes were removed, showing clearly where early doorways had been placed opposite nearby windows. By general agreement the existing, though awkward, arrangement was left in place after original conditions had been documented.

The second surprise at Pavilion III involved alterations that had been made to the upper stair landing. For many years a bathroom had existed on that landing, thereby blocking light that would otherwise have brightened the stairway. Because the second floor required two full bathrooms, the landing had been enclosed some years ago. The possibility of reopening the landing was thoroughly analyzed, but it was concluded that the bathroom would have to remain for the present. The interesting note had to do not with current

72. Pavilion III: restoration of wood entablature and applied lead decoration, 1984. (Photograph by Michael Bailey.)

conditions but with a turn-of-the-century change no longer extant. Mrs. Walter Klingman, who had lived in Pavilion III as a child, heard of the restoration and the discussion of bathrooms. She remembered the stair when it was still open, and also recalled that her father, Professor Raleigh Colston Minor, had built the building's first bathroom as an appendage to the stair landing that protruded through the west window. Upon examination of brickwork in that area, it became clear that a structure had been built, then removed. Without Mrs. Klingman's oral history, we might never have uncovered the facts.[5]

The most noteworthy discovery of recent times occurred in 1987 and involved Pavilion X. Attempts to correct a simple leak in what appeared to be a very old slate roof led to the uncovering of tin-coated iron roofing consisting of a series of seven-by-ten-inch plates. These unusual plates could have represented a significant archaeological find, so we sought an evaluation by Mesick-Cohen-Waite, a specialist in nineteenth-century metal roofing (fig. 73). In the course of their investigation, the firm determined that we had uncovered another of Jefferson's experiments with technologies deriving

from the Industrial Revolution. While metal roofing was not new, Jefferson's method of folding and attaching the plates appears to have been his own invention. Mesick-Cohen-Waite proposed a method of encapsulating the deteriorated historic roofing and reproducing the same technique on top of it, using stainless steel, a more durable metal. Before the work was begun, University craftspersons were trained in appropriate preservation and restoration practices (fig. 74). When the project was completed in 1988, it not only corrected the original physical deterioration, but it also reestablished a forgotten roofing technique. The University was pleased to be of assistance to Monticello by offering this episode as a foundation for a similar, much more complex roofing restoration there that was completed in 1993.

Beginning in 1987 Pavilion I benefitted from the lessons learned at Pavilions VIII and III. Investigative and restoration skills had been well-learned, and it was felt that there would no surprises, but that assumption was mis-

73. Pavilion X: removal of slate to reveal tin-coated iron roofing materials installed by Jefferson's workmen, 1987. (Photograph by Clay Palazzo.)

taken. Study of surviving remnants of early window-frames at the rear of the present first-floor parlor and dining room uncovered tracks for sashes hidden behind bookcases. The windows had originally opened out onto a garden but had been blocked by a nineteenth-century addition; although the sashes had been destroyed, most of the framing had survived. The Design Committee was thus faced with a dilemma: Should the blocked openings be obliterated, or should the original nature of the room somehow be indicated? After studying many alternatives, the Committee recommended that replicas of two of the windows be fabricated and installed. Not only is this strategy commonly used in classical buildings, but it had also been legitimized by Jefferson's own writings.[6] Therefore it seemed fitting to use this concept in order to show the essential nature of the original parlor, even though one can no longer glimpse a garden beyond (fig. 75).

74. Pavilion X: replication of Jefferson's roofing technology using terne-coated stainless steel, 1988. (Photograph by Clay Palazzo.)

The real surprise at Pavilion I came from paint research, which provided an aesthetic jolt. For the first time since paint analysis of the Pavilions had begun in 1985, we had to reexamine the wisdom of our philosophy of color use. Both the front hall and stair hall showed clear evidence of an original yellow so intense that it became light orange under certain lighting conditions. Up to this time the reestablishment of exact tonalities had been considered crucial to the authenticity and professionalism of the program. Now we had to ask ourselves: Is wall color a crucial archaeological concern or is it simply a decorating issue? Debates were enthusiastic and helpful, and ultimately we adopted a position stressing the need for authenticity tempered by

a measure of understanding. The architectural envelope, including paints, should be restored as authentically as possible, but there could be some negotiation in later additions or in upper-floor private areas as long as the overall palette were kept in mind; and inhabitants would be allowed to exercise personal taste in furnishings and artwork.[7] The emphasis on authenticity was based upon the certainty that the buildings, as international monuments, should be viewed as exemplars of their time; as such they must be true to the historical facts even while they must serve as comfortable homes and usable, quasi-public buildings.

The other authors of this book have often mentioned discrepancies between early drawings and the buildings as they were finally constructed. Pavilion VI, the object of restoration between 1989 and 1991, is a perfect example of this phenomenon. An early sketch of the first floor shows a central chimney mass flanked by entry vestibules and two large rooms (fig. 31). By 1989 the building had come to resemble this arrangement, with minor discrepancies. However, study of the woodwork and flooring, as well as the comments of those who knew the building prior to the 1950s, revealed that the center of the building had been open with a central corridor extending from the front door to the rear. As had been the case at Pavilion III, practical considerations won out, and today Pavilion VI remains very much altered and closed. Nevertheless, it is satisfying to the Design Committee to have the record of changes so clearly described.

On the second floor a different situation emerged. The Committee had to decide the fate of a set of frescoes that had been installed in the original sitting room in 1929. The paintings depict historical scenes and personages identified with the early years of the Republic, and with the close relationships between France, the new nation, and Jefferson; however, while they seemed historically suitable, they were not of the highest artistic merit. Again, the

answer came from the imperative to maintain archaeological integrity. The principal recommendation was to conserve the paintings as elements of the life history of the place, an appropriate solution considering their subject matter and the fact that the building had been used since 1960 for the teaching of Romance languages. In response to the decision to adopt the recommendation, a summer training session was held for selected student interns in order to provide field experience in conservation work. Led by internationally known fresco conservator Paul Schwartzbaum, this laboratory exercise was yet another example of a hands-on restoration program that remains unique among American universities.[8]

The most recent restoration, at Pavilion V, illustrates well the informational gaps common to the history of the pavilions. Since the 1820s alterations have typically been made piecemeal, with no attendant written description or drawings describing the scope of work or reasons for changes. Records do mention construction at the west side of Pavilion V as early as about 1829.[9] It was amended over the years, most recently in 1928 with the addition of a segment between the two larger masses (fig. 76).[10] However, several other periods of change that are obvious from examination of the building fabric are not recorded, particularly three or more phases of alteration in the middle zone. For example, stairs were hidden behind closets or cabinetwork; windows were embedded within walls; wall surfaces once exterior became interior; and walls were blocked off so that doors led nowhere. Such mysteries confound preservationists, and they clearly reinforce the beliefs that past evidence and present change must be fully documented and that it is appropriate to leave portions of each puzzling clue intact in the hope that future preservationists will find the answers. Now, workers encapsulate the undocumented feature behind a new surface or beneath layers of protective varnish, analogous to the encapsulation of early roofing materials or graining evidence. Although it had no doubt been covered over for reasons of expediency rather than preservation, the rear garden doorway of Pavilion V was retained in just this manner, awaiting our discovery of it in 1992 (fig. 77).

75. Pavilion I: modifications of a closed window using mirrored glass to reestablish the original image of a window in the west wall of the present parlor, 1988. (Photograph by Clay Palazzo.)

76. Pavilion V: view from the south showing segments, left to right, dating to ca.1829ff, 1928, and ca. 1823. (Photograph by University of Virginia Department of Biomedical Communications.)

77. Pavilion V: removal of plaster to reveal original garden doorway, 1992. (Photograph by Ashley Robbins.)

THE FUTURE

Since 1989 the Jeffersonian Restoration Advisory Board and the Design Committee have been studying options for the Academical Village beyond the year 2000. The activity of the past decade has touched many of Jefferson's buildings but has been concentrated at just over half of the pavilions. Major work remains for the other pavilions, the hotels, and the student rooms. Eventually even the Rotunda, already transformed by two major epochs of redesign, will require more attention. Indeed, the cycle of restoration can never be considered finite, because the University's buildings and landscape are always aging.

The principles that should guide architectural stewardship are based on the belief that no generation should assume that its solutions or attitudes are, for all time, the only right ones. Work should therefore be based on research; and changes, when made, should be gentle and reversible, always leaving the basic historic image intact. Once a major program has been accomplished,

episodes of minor alteration—occurring about every ten years—should be gentle indeed. All the while, allowing for the constant processes of aging and decay, intermittent maintenance is essential. The sum of all these actions serves but one goal: to pass along safely to future generations this phenomenal cultural artifact, which has survived as a gift to this age from the past.

Sustaining and reunifying Jefferson's aspirations for the Academical Village involves more than sound research, more than the physical processes of preservation, conservation, and restoration. There is a profound intellectual component. One must understand Paul Goldberger's comment that "of all the truly great pieces of architecture in this country, [Jefferson's Academical Village] is the most American, the one that best embodies our tendency both to look back at other cultures and to try to make something that is entirely our own."[11] Therefore the Academical Village as artifact provides both lesson and catalyst for those who utilize it and for our entire culture, today and in the years to come.

NOTES

EDUCATION AND ARCHITECTURE:
*The Evolution of the University of
Virginia's Academical Village*

1   This short essay is based on eight years of combined research that adds to the research of many other scholars whose work is cited elsewhere in this essay and publication. We are grateful to Charles Brownell, Associate Professor, Virginia Commonwealth University, for sparking our interest and enthusiasm for this research, then for suggesting this project to bring our findings to a more public forum. We are doubly grateful to Richard Guy Wilson, Chairman, Architectural History, School of Architecture, University of Virginia, and to Anthony Hirschel, Director of the Bayly Art Museum and his dedicated staff for sharing our enthusiasm and seeing this project through to completion.

2   Jefferson to Dr. Joseph Priestly, January 27, 1800, in *The Writings of Thomas Jefferson*, eds. A.A. Lipscomb and A.E. Bergh (Washington, D.C.: The Thomas Jefferson Memorial Association, 1905), vol. 10, 146–47 (L&B).

3   For Jefferson's early education, see Dumas Malone, *Jefferson The Virginian*, vol. 1 of *Jefferson and His Time* (Boston: Little, Brown, 1948), 37–112.

4   William Short to John Hartwell Cocke, July 8, 1828, Cocke Papers, Box 55, Special Collections Department, Manuscripts Division, University of Virginia Library (Special Collections cited hereafter as UVA).

5   *The Architecture of A. Palladio: In Four Books*, ed. Giacomo Leoni, 3rd ed. (London, 1742). There were three editions of this book, 1715, 1721, and 1742. Jefferson probably owned the 1742 edition first. Leoni's plates differed considerably from Palladio's in several instances, and there were substantial inaccuracies in the translated text. See William B. O'Neal, *Jefferson's Fine Arts Library: His Selections for the University of Virginia Together with His Own Architectural Books* (Charlottesville: University Press of Virginia, 1976), 247–77 (O'Neal).

6   A. Lawrence Kocher and Howard Dearstyne, "Discovery of Foundations for Jefferson's Addition to the Wren Building," *Journal of the Society of Architectural Historians* 10 (October 1951), 28–31.

7   Jefferson to James Breckenridge, February 15, 1821, in Roy John Honeywell, *The Educational Work of Thomas Jefferson*, vol. 16, Harvard Studies in Education (Cambridge: Harvard University Press, 1931), Appendix K, 264 (Honeywell).

8   Edmund Pendleton to Jefferson, May 11, 1779, in *The Papers of Thomas Jefferson*, ed. Julian P. Boyd, 23 vols. to date (Princeton: Princeton University Press, 1950ff), vol 2, 266 (Boyd). In this letter, Pendleton refers to Jefferson's letter of Dec 18, 1778, saying "…I have been impatient to se [*sic*] what you call your Quixotism for the diffusion of knowledge, a passion raised by it's [*sic*] title and its being yours.…" Boyd reports that Jefferson's letter to Pendleton has not been found. See also, Boyd, vol. 2, 527–33, for a printed copy of the bill, and pp. 534–35 for a detailed discussion of the proposal.

9   Boyd, vol. 2, 527.

10 Ibid., 528.

11 Jefferson to Joseph C. Cabell, February 2, 1816, Jefferson Papers, Mss., Library of Congress, Washington, D.C. (DLC).

12 Boyd, vol. 2, 529–31.

13 Ibid., 535. Bill no. 80, "A Bill for Amending the Constitution of the College of William and Mary, and Substituting More Certain Revenues for Its Support."

14 Thomas Jefferson, *Autobiography of Thomas Jefferson*, introduction by Dumas Malone (New York: Capricorn Books, 1959), 61.

15 Jefferson to Samuel Henley, October 14, 1785, in Boyd, vol. 8, 635.

16 Jefferson to John Banister, Jr., October 15, 1785, in Boyd, vol. 8, 636–37.

17 Jefferson to George Wythe, August 13, 1786, in Boyd, vol. 10, 244–45.

18 *The Writings of Thomas Jefferson*, ed. Paul Leicester Ford, 10 vols. (New York and London: G.P. Putnam's Sons, 1892), vol. 1, 67 (Ford).

19 Jefferson to Joseph Priestly, January 18, 1800, Honeywell, Appendix C, 215–16.

20 Jefferson to DuPont de Nemours, April 12, 1800, in Neil McDowell Shawen, "The Casting of a Lengthened Shadow: Thomas Jefferson's Role in Determining the Site for a State University in Virginia, " Ph. D. Diss., George Washington University, 1980, 93 (Shawen). Shawen reports that DuPont de Nemours had written a 159-page treatise by June. Jefferson to M. Pictet, February 5, 1803, L&B, vol. 10, 355.

21 Jefferson to L.W. Tazewell, January 5, 1805, Jefferson Papers, UVA.

22 Jefferson to the Trustees for the Lottery of East Tennessee College, May 6, 1810, DLC.

23 Paul B. Barringer, James Mercer Garnett, and Rosewell Page, *A History of the University of Virginia: Its History, Influence, Equipment and Characteristics with Biographical Sketches and Portraits of Founders, Benefactors, Officers and Alumni*, two vols. (New York: Lewis Publishing Company, 1904), vol. 1, 27–32 (Barringer).

24 Jefferson to Dr. Thomas Cooper, January 16, 1814, DLC. See also, Shawen, 131–32, where he cited this letter as the evidence for Jefferson's "hidden agenda" to establish a university at Charlottesville.

25 Barringer, vol. 1, 18.

26 Trustees of Albemarle Academy, Minutes, March 25, April 5, and May 3, 1814, Jefferson Papers, UVA (Trustees).

27 Trustees, Minutes, August 19, 1814. Scholars have dated this plan as May 5, 1817, since that date appeared in Fiske Kimball, *Thomas Jefferson, Architect* (Boston: Clara Amory Coolidge, 1916), 75 (Kimball). See Patricia C. Sherwood, "The Mystery Solved: New Dates and a New Perspective on Thomas Jefferson's Architectural Plans for Educational Institutions in Virginia," *Arts in Virginia* 30 (Fall-Winter 1992), 10–25, for additional evidence surrounding the earlier date of this plan.

28 Jefferson to Peter Carr, September 7, 1814, DLC; cited in Honeywell, Appendix E, 222–27.

29 George W. Randolph to Professor Cabell (Dr. James L. Cabell), February 27, 1856, Cabell Papers, UVA.

30 Jefferson to Yancey, January 6, 1816, as cited in Ford, vol. 10, 2.

31 Frank Carr to Governor Wilson Cary Nicholas, March 25, 1816, *Calendar of Virginia State Papers* 10, 437–38.

32 Jefferson to Nicholas, April 2, 1816, as cited in Honeywell, Appendix G.

33 Edmund Bacon [Jefferson's overseer] to Hamil-

ton W. Pierson, as cited in *Jefferson At Monticello* (New York: Scribner's, 1862), 20.

34 Jefferson to James Dinsmore, April 13, 1817, Jefferson Papers, UVA.

35 Board of Visitors, Minutes, May 5, 1817, UVA.

36 For "excellent architect out of books," see B.H. Latrobe to Christian Ignatius Latrobe, June 5, 1805, in *The Papers of Benjamin Henry Latrobe*, microfiche edition, ed. Thomas E. Jeffrey (Clinton, N. J.: James T. White & Co, 1976), 40/E7.

37 Jefferson to Madison, November 15, 1817, DLC.

38 O'Neal, 117–33. O'Neal reports that the copy of the *Parallèle* that Jefferson acquired after selling his library to Congress was sold as lot 723 in the 1829 sale after Jefferson's death (p. 132). There is still uncharted territory on this issue, however, as the actual acquisition dates have not been tied down.

39 Jefferson to Thornton, May 9, 1817, DLC.

40 Thornton to Jefferson, June 9, 1817, DLC.

41 Jefferson to Latrobe, June 12, 1817, DLC. Charles E. Brownell, in Brownell, Calder Loth, William M.S. Rasmussen, and Richard Guy Wilson, *The Making of Virginia Architecture* (Richmond: Virginia Museum of Fine Arts, 1992), 248, suggests that Thornton's designs did not fit with Jefferson's program to build orthodox models of classical architecture, either, and that "[Thornton's] Doric, for instance, has instead of an architrave and a frieze, a cross between the two, penciled with Adamesque trios of fluting in place of true triglyphs."

42 Latrobe to Jefferson, June 17, 1817, and June 28, 1817, reproduced in *The Correspondence and Miscellaneous Papers of Benjamin Henry Latrobe: Vol 3, 1811–1820*, ed. John C. Van Horne, Series IV, *The Papers of Benjamin Henry Latrobe*, published for the Maryland Historical Society (New Haven: Yale University Press, 1988), vol. 3, 903–06 (Latrobe).

43 Jefferson to Latrobe, July 16, 1817, Latrobe, 907. Jefferson's anxiety about getting Latrobe's drawings may again have resulted from dissatisfaction with Thornton's single scheme and a desire to compare the ideas of both architects before choosing the design for the first pavilion.

44 Jefferson, Specification Book, "Operations at and for the College," July 18, 1817, 3r, UVA.

45 Jefferson to Cocke, July 19, 1817, DLC.

46 Board of Visitors, Minutes, July 28, 1817, Montpelier, Orange, Va., UVA. The minutes refer to: "The plan of the first pavilion to be erected, and the proceedings thereupon, having been stated and agreed to…." This plan was probably executed between July 18 and July 28, as its specifications are recorded after the ground layout in the Specification Book, 3v–5v, UVA. Jefferson meticulously figured the measurements for each minute of the module for his design, and it is the only pavilion design without specifications written on the back of the plan.

47 B.H. Latrobe to Jefferson, July 24, 1817, Latrobe, 914–16.

48 Jefferson to Latrobe, August 3, 1817, DLC. See also, Specification Book, 3v, UVA. Fig. 12 had been attributed by Fiske Kimball as a Jefferson drawing for the White House wings (Kimball, plate 176). However, the interior dimension, fourteen feet, matches that of the other drawings for the University's colonnade; the width of eight feet also matches, as does the Chinese railing above the roof line. None of these measurements on fig. 12 matches those on Jefferson's plan or elevation for the White House wings.

49 By his own admission, Jefferson had executed the 1814 ground plan as an initial concept, and had designed it for economy, convenience, and the ability to be expanded as needed. He had incorporated square columns into the initial scheme for the same reason, saying he would use them "at first." Then, as the hope emerged of having Central College chosen as the University sooner rather than later, he incorporated his own idea of a didactic function for the pavilions, then added the concept of a large central building. The adoption of more elaborate ideas, such as Thornton's proposal for using round, rather than square columns for the colonnade and Latrobe's suggestion for a large Rotunda as the central building, became part of this enlarged concept. However, as his design scheme expanded with outside influence, its emerging form became more and more closely aligned with the design scheme he had used at both Monticello and the White House.

50 Jefferson to Latrobe, October 12, 1817, DLC; Latrobe, 955. An account of laying the corner-stone appeared in the *Richmond Enquirer*, October 10, 1817: "…the first stone of the Central College was laid at Charlottesville on Monday last….The Society of Free Masons, and a large company of citizens attended. The scene was graced by the presence of Thomas Jefferson and James Madison, late Presidents of the United States, and of James Monroe, the actual President."

51 Jefferson to Joseph C. Cabell, October 24, 1817, DLC. A copy of the bill, "A Bill for Establishing A System of Public Education," appears in Honeywell, 233–43. Kimball, 205, identified this plan as a preliminary plan for the University, dating it c. 1804–05. The much later dating of 1817 makes it, instead, an outgrowth of the University Plan, and an optional design for the middle level of education.

52 Jefferson to Joseph Correa de Serra, November 25, 1817, DLC: "mine, after all[,] may be an Utopian dream; but being innocent I have thought I might indulge in it till I go to the land of dreams, and sleep there with the dreamers of all past and future times." Jefferson to Ticknor, November 25, 1817, DLC.

53 Jefferson to Board of Visitors, "Estimate of the objects of application," January 2, 1818, Jefferson Papers, UVA. In his letter to the Trustees of East Tennessee College, May 6, 1810, DLC, Jefferson had suggested the concept of dining students "in smaller & separate Parties" if economically feasible.

54 This conclusion is further supported by the fact that Jefferson told George Ticknor in November that they were "establishing a college of general sciences at … Charlottesville[,] the scale of which, of necessity[,] will be much more moderate." He expected to have ten or twelve professors if the state established it as a university. Jefferson to Ticknor, November 25, 1817, DLC.

55 Joseph C. Cabell to Jefferson, February 20, 1818, Jefferson Papers, UVA.

56 Jefferson to Latrobe, May 19, 1818, DLC.

57 Board of Visitors, Minutes, October 7, 1817, UVA.

58 John Perry to Jefferson, May 26, 1818, Jefferson Papers, Mss., Huntington Library, San Marino, California.

59 Jefferson to Latrobe, May 19, 1818, DLC.

60 The frieze ornament used at Monticello and the University is from the temple of Antoninus and Faustina, from a pattern book by Desgodetz, and can be seen in O'Neal, 94. The use of two different ornament makers resulted in small variations in the two friezes.

61 John Perry to Jefferson, June 18, 1818, Jefferson Papers, UVA.

62 Jefferson to James Madison, June 28, 1818, and to Judge Roane, June 28, 1818, DLC. Jefferson to L.W. Tazewell, June 28, 1818, Jefferson Papers, Mss., Massachusetts Historical Society, Boston.

63 The Rockfish Gap "Report of the Commissioners Appointed to Fix the Site of the University of Virginia, &c." is reproduced in *Early History of the University of Virginia as contained in the letters of Thomas Jefferson and Joseph C. Cabell*, ed. Nathaniel Cabell (Richmond, Va.: J.W. Randolph, 1856), 432ff, and in Honeywell, Appendix J, 248ff. "An Act for establishing an University" appears in the manual of *The Board of Visitors of the University of Virginia* (Charlottesville: University Press of Virginia, 1966).

64 Jefferson to Cocke, March 3, 1819, DLC.

65 "Workmen Wanted," *Richmond Enquirer*, March 23, 1819, UVA. Brockenbrough's arrival is reported in Jefferson to Cabell, March 3, 1819; and his formal appointment on March 29, 1819, is discussed in William B. O'Neal, *Jefferson's Buildings at the University of Virginia: The Rotunda* (Charlottesville: University Press of Virginia, 1960), 19.

66 Jefferson to Richard Ware, April 9, 1819, Jefferson Papers, UVA. A note on the back of this letter in Jefferson's hand gives the number of bricks for the two hotels and the approximate number for Pavilion V (renumbered IX), indicating that he was still in the process of working out the details of this plan.

67 Specifications on the verso of drawing N-330 read: "to correspond with the windows there must be 20. intercolonations...." See Joseph Michael Lasala, "Comparative Analysis: Thomas Jefferson's Rotunda and the Pantheon in Rome," *Virginia Studio Record* 1, no. 2 (1988), 84–87.

68 See Joseph Michael Lasala, "Thomas Jefferson's Designs for the University of Virginia," Master of Architectural History Thesis, University of Virginia, 1992, for a comprehensive analysis of Jefferson's drawings for the University of Virginia.

69 Jefferson to Breckenridge, July 8, 1819, Jefferson Papers, UVA.

70 Joseph C. Cabell to Cocke, April 15, 1819, Cabell Family Papers, UVA . The drawing was definitely completed by April 17, because Cabell told Jefferson in a letter of that date (UVA) that he "… was extremely happy to be informed, by our friend Gen. Cocke, that you had annexed the gardens to the back-yards of the pavilions."

71 Jefferson to Breckenridge, July 8, 1819, UVA. In a letter to Jefferson on May 3 (Jefferson Papers, UVA), Cocke had criticized the second version for not having sufficient gardens for the hotels.

72 Joseph C. Cabell to Cocke, April 15, 1819, Cabell Family Papers, UVA.

73 Cocke to Jefferson May 3, 1819, Jefferson Papers, UVA.

74 Jefferson to Breckenridge, July 8, 1819, Jefferson Papers, UVA.

75 Jefferson to Brockenbrough, June 5, 1819, Proctor's Papers, UVA; and Jefferson to Brockenbrough, June 27, 1819, DLC.

76 "Workmen Wanted," *Richmond Enquirer*, March 23, 1819, UVA.

77 William B. O'Neal, "Michele and Giacomo Raggi at the University of Virginia: With Notes and Documents," *The Magazine of Albemarle County History* 18 (1959–60), 5–31.

78 Brockenbrough to Jefferson, May 1, 1820, Proctor's Papers, UVA.

79 Jefferson to John Wayles Eppes, June 30, 1820, Jefferson Papers, UVA.

80 George W. Spooner to Brockenbrough, March 28, 1821, Proctor's Papers, 141, UVA.

81 Jefferson, Specification Book, 35–6, Jefferson Papers, UVA.

82 Brockenbrough to Jefferson, October 19, 1820, Proctor's Papers, UVA.

83 Brockenbrough to Jefferson, March 29, 1821, Jefferson Papers, UVA.

84 Board of Visitors, Minutes, November 30, 1821, UVA.

85 Edwin Morris Betts, "Ground Plans and Prints of the University of Virginia, 1822–1826," *Proceedings of the American Philosophical Society* 90 (May 1946), 81–90.

86 Jefferson to Breckenridge, July 8, 1819. Jefferson told Breckenridge that he and Cocke had decided to use all the funds for that year on buildings, then call for the annuity of the following year on January 1, which would allow them to have the seven pavilions begun in 1819 completed in 1820. By the spring of 1820, however, the Board of Visitors had determined to finish all ten pavilions and six hotels; Board of Visitors, Minutes, April 3, 1820.

87 Jefferson to Joseph C. Cabell, December 28, 1822, Jefferson Papers, UVA.

88 Neilson to Cocke, February 22, 1823, Cocke Family Papers, UVA. Credit for attributing this and other drawings to Neilson, and not to Jefferson's granddaughter, Cornelia Randolph, goes to C. Allan Brown. At the time of the discovery in 1988, he was working as a consultant to the Center for Palladian Studies.

89 Martha Jefferson Randolph to Nicholas Trist, April 4, 1824, Trist Papers, Southern Historical Collection, University of North Carolina Library, Chapel Hill. Ann M. Lucas of the Thomas Jefferson Memorial Foundation, Charlottesville, kindly shared this reference.

90 Board of Visitors, Minutes, April 5, 1824, UVA.

91 Malone, *The Sage of Monticello*, 402–08 (vol. 6 of *Jefferson and His Time*).

92 Barringer, 93–7. For the pavilion assignments, see Jefferson Papers, [1825], Reel 10. The original list, in Jefferson's hand, is in the James Monroe Memorial Library, Fredericksburg, Va., FC-3084, Acc. 3159.

93 Board of Visitors, Minutes, March 4, 1825, UVA.

94 Edmund Wilcox Hubard to Robert Hubard, June 16, 1826, Hubard Papers, Southern Historical Collection, University of North Carolina Library, Chapel Hill. Thanks go to Rob McDonald, a graduate student in history at the University of North Carolina for sharing this citation.

95 Jefferson to Governor Wilson Cary Nicholas, April 2, 1816, in Honeywell, Appendix G.

JEFFERSON'S LAWN
Perceptions, Interpretations, Meanings

1 This essay is greatly indebted to the many scholars and observers who have written on the University and Thomas Jefferson. Also, I owe thanks to

the many students and colleagues who over the years have discussed the Lawn. I would also like to acknowledge the specific help of Kurt G. F. Helfrich and Martin Perschler who aided with research; for assistance and advice, James Murray Howard, Architect for the Historic Buildings and Grounds, and Thaisa Way, formerly Curator of the Historic Gardens at the University; Barbara Mooney of the University of Illinois; Jennings L. Wagoner, Jr., and Eleanor F. Vernon of the Curry School of Education; Mark R. Wenger of Colonial Williamsburg; Camille Wells of the University of Virginia; and Sidney K. Robinson of the University of Illinois, Chicago.

2   Thomas Jefferson to L.W. Tazewell, Washington, D.C., Jan. 5, 1805, Special Collections, University of Virginia (UVA). See also, Jennings L. Wagoner, Jr., "Jefferson, Justice, and The Enlightened Society" in *Spheres of Justice in Education*, eds. D.A. Verstegen and J.G. Ward (New York: Harper Business, 1971), 11–33.

3   Ticknor to W.H. Prescott, Dec. 16, 1824, cited in George Ticknor, *Life, Letters and Journals of George Ticknor* (Boston: Houghton Mifflin Co., 1909), vol. 1, 348.

4   Jefferson to Cosway, Oct. 24, 1822, in Helen Duprey Bullock, *My Head and My Heart: A Little History of Thomas Jefferson and Maria Cosway* (New York: G. P. Putnam's Sons, 1945), 182; Jefferson to [William Short], Nov. 24, 1821, in *The Writings of Thomas Jefferson*, eds. A.A. Lipscomb and A.E. Bergh (Washington, D.C.: Thomas Jefferson Memorial Association, 1905), vol. 18, 315.

5   Jefferson to Judge Augustus B. Woodward, April 3, 1825, in *The Writings of Thomas Jefferson*, ed. Paul Leicester Ford (New York: G.P. Putnam's Sons, 1892–99), vol. 10, 342.

6   Karl Bernhard, Duke of Saxe-Weimar-Eisenach, *Travels through North America during the years 1825 and 1826*, American edition (Philadelphia: Carey, Lea, and Carey, 1828), 196–201.

7   Quoted in John E. Semmes, *John H.B. Latrobe and His Times, 1803–1891* (Baltimore: Norman, Remington Co., [1917]), 246.

8   Harriet Martineau, *Retrospect of western travel* (London: Saunders and Otley, 1838), vol. 2, 21–23, 32.

9   The basic study is: William B. O'Neal, "An Intelligent Interest in Architecture, A Bibliography of Publications about Thomas Jefferson as an Architect together with an Iconography of the Nineteenth-Century Prints of the University of Virginia," *The American Association of Architectural Bibliographers, Papers* 6 (1969), v-131.

10 Ibid., 75–80; and Edwin M. Betts, "Ground Plans and Prints of the University of Virginia, 1822–1826," *Proceedings of the American Philosophical Society* 90 (May 1946), 81–90.

11 For admiring comments see, William B. O'Neal, *Pictorial History of the University of Virginia* (Charlottesville: University Press of Virginia, 1968), 54. See also, John Hammond Moore, "That 'Commodious' Annex to Jefferson's Rotunda," *Virginia Cavalcade* 29 (Autumn 1979), 114–23.

12 Porte Crayon [David H. Strother], "Virginia Illustrated…," *Harper's New Monthly Magazine* 13 (August 1856), 303–23; reprinted in *Virginia Illustrated: containing a visit to the Virginian canaan and the adventure of Porte Crayon and his cousins* (New York: Harper and Brothers, 1857), 242.

13 Merrill D. Peterson, *The Jefferson Image in the American Mind* (New York: Oxford University Press, 1960), 209.

14 Francis Lister Hawks, *Narrative of events connected with the rise and progress of the Protestant Episcopal Church in Virginia* (New York: Harper, 1836), 21.

15 R.L. Dabney to G. Woodson Payne, Jr., March 18, 1840, Dabney Family Papers, UVA.

16 Reverend William Meade, *Sermon Delivered in the Rotunda of the University of Virginia on Sunday, May 24, 1829* (Charlottesville: F. Carr & Co., 1829), 21.

17 George Tucker to Joseph C. Cabell, March 18, 1835, Cabell Family Papers, UVA. I am indebted for information on the various schemes for chapels to: David A. Dashiell III, "Between Earthy Wisdom and Heavenly Truth: The Effort to Build a Chapel at the University of Virginia, 1835–1890," M.A. Thesis, University of Virginia, 1992.

18 John Hartwell Cocke to Joseph C. Cabell, February 7, 1839, UVA.

19 M. Robert Allen, "A History of the Young Men's Christian Association at the University of Virginia," unpublished paper, UVA.

20 In addition to those cited in this essay, see O'Neal, *Pictorial History*, 63, for a proposed hut for a statue of Jefferson by Alexander Galt and J.L. Cabell; and *Corks and Curls* 6, 170, for a proposed Memorial Arch by Carpenter & Peebles.

21 *Virginia University Magazine* (November 1860), 88.

22 *American Architect and Building News* 29 (November 15, 1885), 240.

23 De Vere, *An Address delivered on the Occasion …* (Charlottesville: Jefferson Book and Job Printing House, 1885), n.p.

24 John C. Kilgo, President of Trinity College (now Duke University), claimed that the University was part of Jefferson's long-range plan for the subversion of Christianity ("A bold enterprise and deistic daring of enormous proportions") in *A Study of Thomas Jefferson's Religious Belief* (Durham, N.C.: n.p., [1900]), 13.

25 William Dunlap, *History of the Rise and Progress of The Arts of Design in The United States* (New York: George P. Scott, 1834), vol. 2, 221–22.

26 Maximilian Schele de Vere, "Mr. Jefferson's Pet," *Harper's New Monthly Magazine* 44 (May 1872), 815–26.

27 Peterson, *The Jefferson Image*, 242.

28 Herbert Baxter Adams, *Thomas Jefferson and the University of Virginia* (Washington, D. C.: Government Printing Office, 1888), 16.

29 Ibid., 16–19.

30 John Kevan Peebles, "Thomas Jefferson, Architect," *American Architect and Building News* 47 (January 19, 1895), 29–30; reprinted from "Thos. Jefferson, Architect," *Alumni Bulletin [University of Virginia]* 1 (November 1894), 68–74. Fayerweather appears in *American Architect* 43, no. 897 (March 4, 1893), n.p. There is much misinformation on Peebles; his correct dates are 1866–1934; I am indebted to the research of David A. Dashiell III on this issue.

31 Charles McKim to William M. Thornton, August 6, 1890, McKim, Mead & White Collection, The New-York Historical Society; McKim to Augustus Saint-Gaudens, May 6, 1895, McKim Collection, Library of Congress; and William R. Mead to Dr. A.H. Buckmaster, November 5, 1895, Proctor's Papers, UVA. See: George Humphrey Yetter, "Stanford White at the University of Virginia: The

NOTES

New Buildings on the South Lawn and the Reconstruction of the Rotunda in 1896," M.A. Thesis, University of Virginia, 1980; and his "Stanford White at the University of Virginia: Some New Light on an Old Question," *Journal of the Society of Architectural Historians* 40 (December 1981): 320–25.

32 Omer Allen Gianniny, Jr., "The Rotunda that was not Built: Mr. Jefferson's Pet Cast in Iron," *The Magazine of Albemarle County History* 40 (1982), 63–88.

33 Report of the Faculty to the Rector and Board of Visitors, October 31, 1895, in *Minutes of the General Faculty* 14 (September 15, 1895–June 15, 1899), 107–11; see Philip Alexander Bruce, *History of the University of Virginia* (New York: MacMillan, 1920), vol. 4, 267–70.

34 [Stanford White], "Notes on the University of Virginia," typescript, ca. 1896, The New-York Historical Society. Slightly rewritten, this was published as Stanford White, "The Buildings of the University of Virginia," *Corks & Curls* 11 (1898), 127–30.

35 Edward Simmons, *From Seven to Seventy* (New York: Harper, 1922), 241.

36 [Stanford White], "Notes on the University of Virginia"; and subsequent quotes in this paragraph.

37 Report of the Faculty, 107–11; Bruce, *History of the University of Virginia*, vol. 4, 268.

38 White to W.M. Thornton [Faculty President], February 26, 1896, Buildings and Grounds Collection, UVA.

39 Jefferson to Governor W.C. Nicholas, April 2, 1816; reprinted in Roy J. Honeywell, *The Educational Work of Thomas Jefferson* (Cambridge: Harvard University Press, 1931), 231.

40 McKim, Mead & White, "Report of the Architects to the Building Committee," March 20, 1895, *Alumni Bulletin of the University of Virginia* 2 (February 1896), 139. (The actual date of the article was 1896, but the Alumni Bulletin mis-dated it and did not publish it until late in 1896.)

41 Plans and views are in *A Monograph of the Works of McKim, Mead & White, 1879–1915* (1915–20; reprint, New York: Dover, 1990 [ed. R.G. Wilson]), pls. 110–112a.

42 As early as 1883 Jefferson rated a mention by Schuyler; see his "Recent Building in New York," *Harper's Magazine* 68 (September 1883), 557–

78; reprinted as "Concerning Queen Anne," in Montgomery Schuyler, *American Architecture and Other Writings*, ed. W. Jordy and R. Coe (Cambridge: Harvard University Press, 1961), 458–59.

43 Montgomery Schuyler, "A History of Old Colonial Architecture," *Architectural Record* 4 (January-March 1895), 351–53.

44 Montgomery Schuyler, "Architecture of American Colleges, VIII: The Southern Colleges," *Architectural Record* 30 (July 1911), 69–79.

45 Glenn Brown, *History of the United States Capital* (Washington, D.C.: U.S. Government Printing Office, 1900–03), vol. 1, 97; and Brown, "Letters from Thomas Jefferson and William Thornton, Architect, Relating to the University of Virginia," *Journal of the American Institute of Architects* 1 (January 1913), 21–27.

46 On the continuing question of authorship, see: Norman M. Isham, "Jefferson's Place in Our Architectural History," *Journal of the American Institute of Architects* 2 (May 1914), 230–35; and Helen M. Gallagher, *Robert Mills, Architect of the Washington Monument, 1781–1855* (New York: Columbia University Press, 1935), 46.

47 William A. Lambeth and Warren H. Manning, *Jefferson as an Architect and Designer of Landscape* (Boston: Houghton Mifflin, 1913), 31.

48 Fiske Kimball, *Thomas Jefferson, Architect* (Boston: Clara Amory Coolidge, 1916).

49 Joseph Die Lehandro, "Fiske Kimball: American Renaissance Historian," M.A. Thesis, University of Virginia, 1982; and George and Mary Roberts, *Triumph on Fairmount: Fiske Kimball and the Philadelphia Museum of Art* (Philadelphia: J.B. Lippincott, 1959).

50 Fiske Kimball, *Thomas Jefferson, Architect* (1916), 80, 81, 82–83.

51 Kimball listed some of the books; the standard list is William B. O'Neal, *Jefferson's Fine Arts Library: His Selections for the University of Virginia Together with His Own Architectural Books*, (Charlottesville: University Press of Virginia, 1976); see also, O'Neal, *A Fine Arts Library: Jefferson's Selections for the University of Virginia Together with His Architectural Books at Monticello* (exhibition catalogue, Charlottesville: University of Virginia, 1976).

52 Fiske Kimball, "Thomas Jefferson and the First Monument of the Classic Revival in America," *Journal of the American Institute of Architects* 3 (September, October, November, 1915), 370–81, 421–33, 473–91; and Kimball, "Thomas Jefferson and the Origin of the Classical Revival in America," *Art and Archaeology* 1 (May 1915), 219–27.

53 Kimball, *Thomas Jefferson, Architect*, 78; see also, Susan D. Riddick, "The Influence of B.H. Latrobe on Jefferson's Design for the University of Virginia," M. A. Thesis, University of Virginia, 1988, 30–33, which conveniently summarizes the various positions.

54 The book owned by Jefferson is, J. Ch. Krafft and Pierre Nicholas Ransonnette, *Plans, coupes, èlevations des plus belles maisons et des hôtels construits à Paris et dans les environs* (Paris, [1801–03]). For historians, see: William H. Pierson, Jr., "The Colonial and Neo-Classical Styles" in *American Buildings and Their Architects* (Garden City: Doubleday, 1970), 329–33; Frederick D. Nichols, "Jefferson: The Making of an Architect," in W.H. Adams, ed., *Jefferson and the Arts: An Extended View* (Washington, D.C.: National Gallery of Art, 1976), 169, 173–74; and William Howard Adams, ed., *The Eye of Thomas Jefferson* (Washington, D.C.: National Gallery of Art, 1976), 293, note by Nichols.

55 Jefferson had seen William Kent's Temple of Venus at Stowe during his English trip of 1786, and he apparently owned B. Seeley, *Stowe: A Description of the Magnificent House and Gardens* (London, 1783). On the Roman connection, see Charles Brownell, "Laying the Groundwork" in Brownell, Loth, Rasmussen, and Wilson, *The Making of Virginia Architecture* (Richmond: Virginia Museum of Fine Arts, 1992), 52 and 56ff.

56 Kimball, *Thomas Jefferson, Architect*, 80.

57 Fiske Kimball, "The Genesis of Jefferson's Plan for the University of Virginia," *Architecture* 48 (December 1923), 397–99.

58 In addition to Nichols's writings cited in n. 54, see: Frederick Doveton Nichols, *Thomas Jefferson's Architectural Drawings* (Boston: Massachusetts Historical Society, and Charlottesville: Thomas Jefferson Memorial Foundation and University Press of Virginia, 1961), 8.; and Albert Bush-

Brown, "College Architecture," *Architectural Record* 122 (August 1957), 156.

59 William B. O'Neal, "Origins of the University Ground Plans," *Alumni News* 50 (November 1962), 4–7; Mary Woods, "Thomas Jefferson and the University of Virginia: Planning the Academic Village," *Journal of the Society of Architectural Historians* 44 (October 1985), 266–83; Walter L. Creese, *The Crowning of the American Landscape: Eight Great Spaces and Their Buildings* (Princeton: Princeton University Press, 1985), 16–21; Bryan Little, "Cambridge and the Campus: An English Antecedent for the Lawn of the University of Virginia," *Virginia Magazine of History and Biography* 79 (April 1971), 190–201; Christopher Tunnard, "Jean-Jacques Ramée," *Union Worthies* 19 (1964), 12–13.

60 Paul Venable Turner, *Campus: An American Planning Tradition* (New York: The Architectural History Foundation, 1984), 79–83; David Bell, "Knowledge and the Middle Landscape: Thomas Jefferson's University of Virginia," *Journal of Architectural Education* 37 (Winter 1983), 18–26.

61 Vincent Scully, *American Architecture and Urbanism* (New York: Praeger, 1969), 54, 57–60.

62 Cranston Jones, "Pride and Prejudices of the Master," *Life* 46 (April 27, 1959), 56.

63 Lewis Mumford, *The South in Architecture* (New York: Harcourt, Brace & Co., 1941), 70–76.

64 Stanislaw Makielski, a professor in the Architecture Department, directed the work; Fiske Kimball acted as a consultant.

65 Many of O'Neal's and Nichols's publications are cited elsewhere. See also, William Bainter O'Neal, *Jefferson's Buildings at the University of Virginia: The Rotunda* (Charlottesville: University Press of Virginia, 1960); O'Neal and Nichols, "An Architectural History of the First University Pavilion," and O'Neal, "The Workmen at the University of Virginia 1817–1826 with Notes and Documents," "Michele and Giacomo Raggi at the University of Virginia: With Notes and Documents," and "Financing the Construction of the University of Virginia: Notes and Documents," all in *The Magazine of Albemarle County History* 15, 17, 18, 23 (1957, 1958–59, 1959–60, 1964–65), 36–43, 5–48, 5–31, 4–34.

66 Fiske Kimball, *American Architecture* (Indianapolis and New York: Bobbs-Merrill, 1928), 178–79. Bruce, *History of the University of Virginia*, vol. 4, 274, 277–79, indicates the praise. In subsequent years other buildings, such as Brooks Hall, have been criticized as being non-conforming; however, they have been successfully preserved.

67 Henry-Russell Hitchcock, *Architecture: Nineteenth and Twentieth Centuries* (Baltimore: Penguin, [1969] 1971), 598, n. 7; see also, Scully, *American Architecture*, 57.

68 The architects were Ballou & Justice of Richmond; Nichols acted as consultant. See: Frederick D. Nichols, "Restoring Jefferson's University" in *Building Early America*, ed. C.E. Peterson (Philadelphia: Carpenter's Company, 1976), 319–39; Virginius Dabney, *Mr. Jefferson's University* (Charlottesville: University Press of Virginia, 1981), 574–75; Joseph Lee Vaughan and Omer Allan Gianniny, Jr., *Thomas Jefferson's Rotunda Restored, 1973–76* (Charlottesville: University Press of Virginia, 1981); and "Towards a Restored Rotunda," and Francis L. Berkeley, Jr., "Mr. Jefferson's Rotunda: Myths and Realities," *University of Virginia Alumni News* 56 (May-June, 1966), 6–9, and 60 (July-August, 1972), 5–9.

69 Peter Blake, *God's Own Junkyard* (New York: Holt, Rinehart Winston, 1964), 32–33; an "ironical" twist that pointed out the "irrelevancy of the comparison" is Robert Venturi, *Complexity and Contradiction in Architecture* (New York: Museum of Modern Art, 1966), 102–03.

70 "Highlights of American Architecture," *AIA Journal* 65 (July 1976), 88–158.

71 Sermon by the Reverend Jerry Falwell, Lynchburg, Virginia, October 11, 1987.

72 Merrill Peterson, "Introduction," *The Portable Jefferson* (New York: Viking Press, 1975), xi-xii; Karl Lehmann, *Thomas Jefferson, American Humanist* (1947; reprint, Charlottesville: University Press of Virginia, 1985), 164.

73 Jefferson to John Adams, October 28, 1813, in Peterson, *The Portable Jefferson*, 539.

74 Jefferson to William Ludlow, September 6, 1824, in Peterson, *The Portable Jefferson*, 583–84.

75 Jefferson to John Adams, July 5, 1814, and Nov. 7, 1819, in Padover, *The Complete Jefferson*, 1034–38.

76 Jefferson to editor of the *Journal de Paris*, August 29, 1787, "Notes on the State of Virginia," 1781–85; and Report of the Commissioners for the University of Virginia," August 1–4, 1818, in Padover, *The Complete Jefferson*, 74, 668, 1099.

77 Jefferson to Tazewell, January 5, 1805, UVA.

78 The frequent claim that Jefferson viewed Palladio as a "bible" comes only from a second-hand source; see the letter of I.A. Coles to General John Hartwell Cocke, February 23, 1816, Cocke Papers, UVA.

79 Dumas Malone, *The Sage of Monticello*, vol. 6 of *Jefferson and His Time* (Boston: Little Brown, 1948), 498–99.

80 Information on Jefferson's time at the College is in Malone, *Jefferson the Virginian*, chp. 4 (vol. 1 of *Jefferson and His Time*); on the building, see James Kornwolf, *"So Good a Design," The Colonial Campus of the College of William and Mary: Its History, Background, and Legacy* (Williamsburg: College of William and Mary, Muscarelle Museum of Art, 1989). I have benefited from talks with Mark Wenger of Colonial Williamsburg on this topic.

81 Except for the few students who chose to board in town, of which Jefferson was not included.

82 Malone, *Jefferson the Virginian*, 44 (vol. 1 of *Jefferson and His Time*), disagrees on this point with Fawn M. Brodie, *Thomas Jefferson: An Intimate History* (New York: W.W. Norton, 1974), 54–55.

83 Thomas Jefferson, "Notes on the State of Virginia" in Peterson, *The Portable Jefferson*, 200, 203.

84 Tutwiler quoted in Bruce, *History of the University of Virginia*, vol. 2, 300.

85 Jennings L. Wagoner, Jr. "Honor and Dishonor at Mr. Jefferson's University: The Antebellum Years," *History of Education Quarterly* 26 (Summer 1986), 155–80.

86 Jefferson to Cabell, December 28, 1822, in Cabell, *Early History of the University of Virginia* (Richmond: J.W. Randolph, 1856), 260–61.

87 Malone, *The Sage of Monticello*, 369 (vol. 6 of *Jefferson and His Time*).

88 Jefferson, "Political Science," March 4, 1825, in Padover, *The Complete Jefferson*, 1112; Malone, *The Sage of Monticello*, 417 (vol. 6 of *Jefferson and His Time*).

89 Mark R. Wenger, "Thomas Jefferson, Tenant,"

NOTES

Winterthur Portfolio 26 (Winter 1991), 249–65.

90 Jefferson to Governor William C. Claiborne, July 7, 1804, in Peterson, *The Portable Jefferson*, 499–500.

91 See Jefferson's letters to: Jean Baptiste Say, February 1, 1804; John Adams, October 28, 1813; and Benjamin Austin, January 9, 1816. See also, his "Notes" in Peterson, *The Portable Jefferson*, 217, 227, 497–99, 539, 547–50.

92 Jefferson to Dr. Caspar Wistar, June 21, 1807, in Padover, *The Complete Jefferson*, 1060.

93 Jefferson to L.W. Tazewell, January 5, 1805, UVA.

94 For references to plantations as villages, see: Antonio Pace, ed. and trans., *Luigi Castiglioni's Viaggio: Travels in the United States of America, 1785–1787* (Syracuse, N.Y.: Syracuse University Press, 1983), 193–94; Thomas Anburey, *Travels Through the Interior Parts of America [1776–81]* (Boston: Houghton Mifflin Co, 1923), vol. 2, 187; and Johann David Schoepf, *Travels in the Confederation [1788]* (Philadelphia: William J. Campbell, 1911), vol. 2, 32–33. Camille Wells kindly helped me with these sources.

95 Lehmann, *Thomas Jefferson, American Humanist* (1947; reprint, Charlottesville: University Press of Virginia, 1985), 180–85.

96 The number of possible European prototypes is very large. John Harris recently showed me a scheme by the British amateur Ambrose Phillipps for the Place Royale, Montpellier, dating from c. 1735 that has striking similarities with the Lawn; however, there is no evidence, and it is extremely doubtful that Jefferson knew of it. The drawings for Phillipps's scheme are in the Royal Institute of British Architects collection.

97 Vincent Scully, *New World Visions of Household Gods & Sacred Places* (Boston: New York Graphic Society, Little Brown, 1988), 70.

98 Lehmann, *Thomas Jefferson, American Humanist*, 157, 163.

99 Jefferson to Latrobe, June 12, 1817, Library of Congress.

100 Lehmann, *Thomas Jefferson, American Humanist*, 165.

101 Many scholars have noted Jefferson's interest in these forms. Jefferson originally introduced the idea in his "Account of the Capitol in Virginia" [ca. 1793–97], reprinted in Fiske Kimball, *The Capitol of Virginia*, ed. Jon Kukla (Richmond: Virginia State Library and Archives, 1989), 13.

102 A[ndrea]. Palladio, *The Architecture of A. Palladio … Revis'd, Design'd, and Publish'd by Giacomo Leoni*, 2d ed. (London: 1721), vol. 2, bk. 4, 74, claimed that the body of the Pantheon "was erected in the time of the *Republick*." Jefferson himself claimed that the "Maison quarree [was] erected in the time of the Caesars," in a letter dated January 26, 1787, reprinted in Kimball, *The Capitol of Virginia*, 22.

103 Palladio, *Architecture*, vol. 2, bk. 4, 74. Malone, *The Sage of Monticello*, 386 (vol. 6 of *Jefferson and His Time*).

104 Jefferson, "Account of the Capitol …" in Kimball, *The Capitol of Virginia*, 13.

105 Palladio, *Architecture*, vol. 2, bk. 4, 74.

106 Lehmann, *Thomas Jefferson, American Humanist*, 187; Jefferson, Specification Book, July 18, 1819, 3, UVA.

107 Pointed out by Riddick, "Influence of B.H. Latrobe," 44; see Vitruvius Pollio, *Les dix livres d'architecture de Vitruve corrigez et traduits nouvellement en françois, avec des notes et des figures*, trans. Claude Perrault (Paris: J.B. Coignard, 1684), bk. 3, chp. 1, pl. 7. Jefferson acknowledged the Perrault volume—though not the plate—in a letter to Isaac McPherson, August 13, 1813, as cited in Peterson, *The Portable Jefferson*, 527.

108 The first four numbers—I-III on the west, and II-IV on the east—are 53 feet and 64 feet apart respectively. Number V on the west is 89 feet from III, and number VI on the east is 90.5 feet from IV. The next on the west, VII, is 104 feet, then IX is 122 feet, and for the east, numbers VIII and X, nearly the same dimensions hold. The small differences between the east and west dimensions result from the different widths of the pavilions. Lambeth and Manning, *Jefferson as an Architect and Designer of Landscape*, 62, gave measurements that were wrong; Creese, *The Crowning of the American Landscape*, 28, provided more correct versions. My dimensions were provided by James Murray Howard, AIA, Architect for the Historic Buildings and Grounds.

109 Kimball, *Thomas Jefferson, Architect*, 82; see also, Marvin Trachtenberg and Isabelle Hyman, *Architecture* (New York: Abrams, 1986), 443.

THE ACADEMICAL VILLAGE TODAY

1 *The World Heritage Convention* (Washington, D.C.: United States Committee/International Council on Monuments and Sites, 1992), 1. The World Heritage List, begun in 1978, recognizes properties of exceptional and universal cultural significance throughout the world. In 1992 the list contained 358 sites in eighty-two countries; seventeen of the sites are in the United States.

2 *ICOMOS: 1964–1984* (Paris: International Council on Monuments and Sites, 1983), 79–83.

3 Mesick-Cohen-Waite Architects, *Pavilion V* (Albany, N.Y.: Mount Ida Press, 1993).

4 *Comprehensive Plan for Residential Life* (Charlottesville: Committee on Residential Life, University of Virginia), 34–35.

5 Author's interview with Mrs. Walter Klingman, June 27, 1986. Mrs. Klingman lived in Pavilion III between 1904 and 1923. Her father was a professor of law.

6 Design Committee, Jeffersonian Restoration Advisory Board, University of Virginia, Minutes, Dec. 16, 1987, March 2, 1988, and April 5, 1988.

7 Ibid., March 2, 1988.

8 Ibid., March 30 and September 29, 1989.

9 Board of Visitors, Minutes, July 20, 1829ff, UVA. Entries record several changes at Pavilion V, beginning as early as 1829, but do not offer sufficient detail to clarify the date for any specific segment of the alterations.

10 Tripp Evans, "Pavilion V," *The Cavalier Daily*, October 24, 1988, 5.

11 Paul Goldberger, "Jefferson's Legacy: Dialogues With the Past," *The New York Times*, May 23, 1993, H33. Goldberger is the *Times*'s architectural critic.

INDEX

INDEX

92